18 Destiny Helpers You Need

Other Publications By The Author

1. 21 Days Prayer Power for a Great Turnaround
   2020 Paperback
2. Be an Encourager Workbook
   2019 Paperback
3. Your 4 Fathers and their Kingdoms
   2018 Paperback/Hardcover
4. Oasis of Elim: 31 Day Devotional
   2018 Paperback
5. Be an Encourager
   2017 Paperback/E-Book
6. Spiritual Leadership For the Next Generation
   2013 Paperback
7. Right Leadership - Making Impact Today!
   2013 Paperback/E-Book

18 Destiny Helpers You Need

James Fadel

Published By:

Fadel Publishing
Greenville (Dallas), TX
USA

Copyright © **James Fadel**, June 2022

All rights reserved. No part of this book should be reproduced or transmitted in any form or by any means- electronic or mechanical, including photocopying, recording, or by any information storage and retrieval system without written permission from the author and the publisher.

All Bible quotations are taken from the King James Version (NKJV) except where stated otherwise.

CATALOGUING-IN PUBLICATION DATA

FADEL, JAMES.
Eighteen Destiny Helpers You Need
1. Christian Life - Biblical Teaching
2. Destiny-actualization - Religious aspect - Christianity
I. Title

BV 595.3.F341   2022

ISBN: 978-0-9960348-3-8   Pbk   AACR

Contact The Author At:
RCCG North America Operations,
515 County Road 1118,
Greenville, TX 75401, U.S.A.
Tel - +(1) 248-240-2641
Email – jfadel2000@yahoo.com

Printed in the United States Of America

Dedication

This book is dedicated to my own Mummy G., Pastor (Mrs.) Folu Adeboye, the wife of the General Overseer of the Redeemed Christian Church of God Worldwide. I am dedicating the book to her in honor of all her humanitarian efforts, both known and unknown. Her globally known humanitarian efforts include, but are not limited to, *Africa Missions Global*, *Friends of Jesus*, *Habitation of Hope*, *Wholistic Outreach*, and an affiliation with *Christ Against Drug Abuse Ministry*.

The purpose of dedicating this book in honor of her efforts is to ensure that all proceeds for the sales of this book goes to support her work with Africa Missions globally. RCCG The Americas is spearheading a US$1 million fundraising campaign for Africa Missions.

Acknowledgments

With sincere gratitude to God, I choose to appreciate the exceeding favor upon my life from finding my wife of almost thirty-three (33) years (Proverbs 18:22). I have been extremely blessed by her gentle spirit, godly counsel, and her commitment to our marriage to the extent that she opted to join me in full-time ministry at the expense of her career as a pediatric physician. Through her, God has blessed me with three wonderful, beautiful, and smart daughters who love the LORD.

Needless to say, I cannot be where I am today in ministry without the mentorship and coaching of my father-in-the-LORD, Pastor E.A. Adeboye, the General Overseer of the Redeemed Christian Church of God Worldwide. It has been, and continues to be, worthwhile following him as he follows Christ (1 Corinthians 11:1).

I also appreciate the tremendous contributions of all those who worked towards the success of this book from behind the scenes. Special gratitude goes to the Editor, Mr. Shafe Ewuola, who labored diligently over this project at every step of the way from inception to publishing. He was ably assisted by many people including my Personal Assistant for Communications, Mrs. Olajumoke Lawal.

To the many people who contributed in their unique way, but for lack of space to mention them all, I say thank you and God bless you. Amen. Ultimately, all thanks belongs to the LORD our God, the Father of heavenly lights who gives good gifts and with Whom there is no shadow of turning (James 1:17). He does not change like shifting shadows, and He has made this project feasible, ensuring that it thrived to fruition. Blessed be His holy Name.

Contents

Dedication	*v*
Acknowledgments	*vi*
Introduction	*x*

Chapter 1
Eighteen Destiny Helpers You Need — 15

Chapter 2
Any Destiny Helper Is God's Tool — 50

Chapter 3
The Christian Is A Special Destiny Helper — 60

Chapter 4
Why Destinies Need Helpers — 70

Chapter 5
When God Uses A Destiny Helper — 82

Chapter 6
When A Destiny Helper Is Under Attack — 88

Chapter 7
**Right Timing With Destiny
Opportunities**   97

Chapter 8
Your Destiny Is Your Purpose   106

Chapter 9
**Every Day Is A New Destiny
Opportunity**   114

Chapter 10
Seven Principles Of Purpose   126

Introduction

An epic illustration of a life without destiny helpers is the meandering story of a bedridden man laid back in the religious and economic hustle and bustle of the Jewish city of Jerusalem. Planted in the plot of Jesus' promotion of a new Kingdom life and its unlimited, all-round insurance benefits for everyone, the man's pathetic story peaks on how his lack of destiny helpers fettered him to a spot for 38 years.

A picture of apparent contradictions pops up as we journey through his story terrain. The poolside to which he had been abandoned for the past 38 years became his circumstantial home. Housed in a territory of fellow invalids, his hope of a better life hung in the balances of providence. John writes that the pool's name, Bethesda, was derived from a root word in either Hebrew or Aramaic. Either one, it was said to mean 'house of mercy' or 'house of grace.'

> *Under a religious atmosphere, nothing changes; but under a spiritual atmosphere that God's Spirit creates, everything changes.*

How mercy or grace eluded this man for 38 years has no further explanation than his own testimony that 'I have no man.' That was his response, submission, argument and story. He was ostracized from the feast in Jerusalem which drew participants, worshippers and probably tourists from across the world. His condition forced him to play audience to the economic activities of sheep merchants in the area. To describe it in modern terms, we would say his social life housed him in the same apartment building full of sick, invalid, bedridden and forsaken folks.

John 5: 1-15 presents the theatrics of empathy through its plot, setting, characters and dialogue. The plot is about Jesus' intervention in the degenerative condition of a man without destiny helpers. Most suitably, the story finds its setting in the religious atmosphere of Jerusalem which was soon to be replaced with a new atmosphere of spiritual power. Under a religious atmosphere, nothing changes; but under a spiritual atmosphere that God's Spirit creates, everything changes. The impotent man and Jesus are the main characters and their dialogue has been the subject of over two thousand years of literary and spiritual exploits.

This man's story both foretold and re-tells subsequent stories of any life without destiny helpers. The plot may slightly differ, the environment may be unrelated, the characters may cut across all boundaries but the dialogue always produces the same result of 'I have no man' or 'I have no destiny helper.' An excerpt from Jesus' dialogue with him in John 5: 6-7 reads, 'When Jesus saw him lying there, and knew that he already had been in that condition a long time, He said to him, "Do you want to be made well?" The sick man answered Him, "Sir, I have no man to put me into the pool when the water is stirred up; but while I am coming, another steps down before me."

Our empathy for this man, through associative feeling with his old story, grows deeper when Jesus acknowledged that 'he already had been in that condition a long time.' Without destiny helpers, problems prolong their lifespans while the victim's lifespan risks being cut short. To Jesus' question that 'Do you want to be made well?' the man had no sense of clear answer anymore. He had no answer but a story to tell – a story of many disappointments and lost opportunities.

His sense of clarity on what he wanted, which should have made him answer either 'Yes' or 'No' had weakened through his poor, declining health condition. Being long without destiny helpers could leave you more confused about what you want when a destiny helper appears. Jesus' question was in the present tense: 'Do you want to be made well?' He asked. But the man's answer was in the past, lost opportunities which have conditioned his present conclusion that 'Sir, I have no man.' It wasn't just a past experience; but what his condition has permanently become.

This story has been told many times but we scarcely pay attention to the fact that the man was not completely without destiny helpers before Jesus appeared to His rescue. Have you asked this question: who brought him to the poolside? Whoever did was a destiny helper. That was the farthest that destiny helper could go but his case needed a further push. His previous story and the characters involved before He met Christ classify the roles of some destiny helpers. They can only take you to the border of your breakthroughs and not any further. To go further, you need another type of destiny helpers.

> *Without destiny helpers, problems prolong their lifespans while the victim's lifespan risks being cut short.*

Classifying destiny helpers according to their roles in different stages of your life is important for you to discern, identify and hook up with the appropriate destiny helpers you need. In this book, I have put together profound guidelines on recognizing 18 types of destiny helpers and how to decode their signs when you meet them. Guess what? Your story will change beyond your expectation after reading this book. I look forward to hearing your testimony pretty soon.

James Fadel
June 2022

1

Eighteen Destiny Helpers You Need

On an island in the Caribbean, off the eastern coast of Mexico's peninsula, two brothers competed in the 2016 edition of the World Triathlon Series (WTS). The event was a series of competitions, building up to the grand finale of crowning an annual and overall world Triathlon champion.

Triathlon is multisport which combines swimming, cycling, and running over different distances. It's an event that has earned itself the title 'an endurance multisport race.' Competitors, known as triathletes, train to gain endurance for swimming, strength for cycling, and speed for running.

The first of the brothers is the famous Alistair Brownlee, a British triathlete and the only athlete to hold two Olympic titles in the event. In the 2012 and 2016 Olympics, he won gold medals, respectively. He is famous as a two-time World Team Champion in 2011 and 2012; a four-time European Champion in 2010, 2011, 2014, and 2019; and the 2014 Commonwealth champion.

His intimidating and flourishing records got all eyes fixed on him at the 2016 Mexico event. But this time, he would not win the gold medal he deserved because he decided to be a destiny helper. Destiny helpers don't always win; they also help others to win.

His brother's name is Jonny Brownlee. Like, Alistair, he too is a professional duathlete and triathlon who won the 2012 Triathlon World Champion and the Silver medal in 2013 and 2016. Comparing their records, Alistair undoubtedly towered above his brother's achievements. At the Mexico event, fans did not expect him to perform less than his previous records. Some of them might have projected he would even beat his past illustrious feats.

The media reported that Jonny was leading the race comfortably, coasting to win the race with just a few kilometers to the finish line. Suddenly, he began to wobble, losing the stamina to stand and complete the race. The opportunity to win the race started waning. He wasn't just going to lose the championship medal; he would probably collapse and end the race with no medal at all, despite being close to the finish line.

Jonny was in the first position toward the finish line before being exhausted and dazed. A competitor from South Africa, Henri Schoeman, was in the second position, and Alistair was cruising behind them in the third position. When Alistair saw his brother zigzagging off the track and staggering to a fall, he sacrificed the chance to outrun him and the South African.

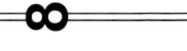

Destiny helpers don't always win; they also help others to win.

He veered off to help his brother across the finish line. Although the South African took the advantage to come first in the race, Alistair ensured he held up his exhausted brother by the waist, and both of them jogged clumsily toward the finish line.

A few inches from the finish line, Alistair did an incredible thing by pushing his brother across the line to finish second while he sacrificially took the third position in a race he possibly could have won.

The punch line of their story is that Alistair 'pushed his brother across the line.' Later, Jonny was said to write an appreciation to his brother on his Twitter handle from his hospital bed, saying, 'Not how I wanted to end the season but gave it everything. Thanks, @AliBrownleetri, your loyalty is incredible."

Different people have reacted to this story from different angles. Some sports enthusiasts blamed Alistair for his action, while others commended his rare demonstration of sportsmanship. Alistair's action of pushing his brother across the finish line captures the definition of a destiny helper. A destiny helper pays the price, sacrifices his resources, gives up his chances, and sometimes forfeits his prize for someone else to win. Anyone willing to push you across the finish line to your destiny fulfillment is a destiny helper.

There are as many destiny helpers as the finish lines to cross. There are clear finish lines to cross in business, ministry, career, marriage, and family life. Like Jonny Brownlee, your preparation, determination, and efforts may take you close to the finish line and still be unable to cross it. Being close to the success finish line does not make you successful; being close to the winning finish line does not make you a winner. You could also be close to your final destination without getting there. You need a destiny helper to push you across the line.

Everyone needs someone. One of the greatest mistakes you could make is to believe that you need everybody to fulfill your dream. You don't need everybody; you need someone to get you somewhere. One step at a time, recognize the type of destiny helper you need and get connected when you meet one. I have enumerated below eighteen types of destiny helpers you should pray to meet.

Take a look at them one by one to prepare your expectation and reshape your appreciation if you have met some of them already. Expectation and appreciation are the two applicable rules when dealing with destiny helpers. Expect to meet them and appreciate the ones you have encountered.

1. Destiny Connector

This type of destiny helper connects you from the bottom to the top. A perfect example is Daniel's recommendation of his three friends - Shadrach, Meshach, and Abednego - to the government he served as a Special Adviser. The four friends were victims of the same circumstance. They were forcefully taken from their country, Israel, to Babylon as captives or slaves.

Meanwhile, they got a scholarship and were listed for a three-year academic program in the highest-ranking Academy of Babylon. The Academy was comparable to today's Harvard in the United States of America, the University Of Oxford in the United Kingdom, the University of Toronto in Canada, the University of Melbourne in Australia, Swiss Federal Institute of Technology in Zurich, Tsinghua University in China, and others according to 2022 USNews on best global university ranking. The reason is that exceptional products of the Academy had automatic placements in the highest government positions in the land.

Daniel and his friends demonstrated rare scholastic aptitude, strict self-discipline, moral uprightness, and strong faith in God. The young guys studied, prayed, and fasted together as occasions demanded. Although they were foreign or international students in Babylon, they all excelled in the Arts faculty. They were ten times better than their native colleagues. Their specialization was in the double majors of linguistics and literature of Babylon.

> *Anyone willing to push you across the finish line to your destiny fulfillment is a destiny helper.*

Following Daniel's additional performance and laurel in a more specialized examination, he was rewarded with the office of a Special Adviser to the King of Babylon. The reward was apart from the gifts, wealth, honor, and stupendous remunerations he enjoyed. After accepting the offer with gratitude, he immediately recommended his three friends for the topmost positions as Governors-General in Babylon's economic and political systems.

Daniel 2: 49 says, '*Also Daniel petitioned the king, and he set Shadrach, Meshach, and Abed-Nego over the affairs of the province of Babylon; but Daniel sat in the gate of the king.*' From the bottom position, Daniel connected his friends to the topmost positions in government. A destiny helper could be a school friend, business colleague, fellow gospel minister, or anyone in the position to pull you up from the bottom.

2. Destiny Facilitator

David's rise to stardom in Israel began with the role of a destiny helper who facilitated his ambition. On his father's errand to his elder brothers on the battlefield, he heard the threat, boasting, and blasphemy of Goliath, the Army General and Combatant Commander (CC) of the Philistine army. Israel and the Philistines were drawn into a prolonged war with no victor and no vanquished.

Hearing the enemy's lousy mockery of the Israeli army and watching his country's military under Saul's command retreating in fear, he expressed interest as a volunteer fighter to take on Goliath. One of his older brothers in the army disdained him, dismissing his ambition as nothing but pride. As he insisted on taking the risk for his country, someone took his message to

King Saul.

1 Samuel 17: 26-31:

26 Then David spoke to the men who stood by him, saying, "What shall be done for the man who kills this Philistine and takes away the reproach from Israel? For who is this uncircumcised Philistine, that he should defy the armies of the living God?"

27 And the people answered him in this manner, saying, "So shall it be done for the man who kills him."

28 Now Eliab his oldest brother heard when he spoke to the men; and Eliab's anger was aroused against David, and he said, "Why did you come down here? And with whom have you left those few sheep in the wilderness? I know your pride and the insolence of your heart, for you have come down to see the battle."

29 And David said, "What have I done now? Is there not a cause?

30 Then he turned from him toward another and said the same thing; and these people answered him as the first ones did.

31 Now when the words which David spoke were heard, they reported them to Saul; and he sent for him.

The King sent for David after he was informed about his boldness and bravery. Whoever conveyed David's words to the King among the soldiers was his destiny helper. He facilitated his meeting with the King, and the remaining part of the story was his sudden rise to stardom following his victory over Goliath. A destiny facilitator paves the way for your meeting with those that matter. He creates the opportunity to demonstrate your gifts and sponsors your ambition to fruition.

3. Destiny Organizer

A destiny organizer is strategically positioned to reposition you. Joseph had a perfect interpretation of God's providence in making him a Prime Minister in Egypt. He told his brothers that God strategically positioned him to reposition the family and their posterity to survive the world's economic recession at that time.

Everyone needs someone.

Genesis 45: 4-8:

4. "Please come near to me." So they came near. Then he said: "I am Joseph your brother, whom you sold into Egypt.

5 "But now, do not therefore be grieved or angry with yourselves because you sold me here; for God sent me before you to preserve life.

6 "For these two years the famine has been in the land, and there are still five years in which there will be neither plowing nor harvesting.

7 "And God sent me before you to preserve a posterity for you in the earth, and to save your lives by a great deliverance.

8 "So now it was not you who sent me here, but God; and He has made me a father to Pharaoh, and lord of all his house, and a ruler throughout all the land of Egypt.

Joseph was a destiny helper who re-organized, repositioned, and relocated his family members from a country with failed economy to a land of greener pasture. God did not put you in your present, strategic position for selfish interests. As you trust God to reposition you through someone else, ask Him to use you to reposition others to fulfill their destiny.

4. Destiny Risk-Taker

Obadiah was a governor in charge of the family affairs of Ahab and his wicked queen, Jezebel. During a severe famine, he was also responsible for heading an Economic Recovery Team. He was to scout for resources to harness them for the country to survive the rapidly failing economy.

His fame was not because of his position with the government of the land. It was not because of his special relationship with the people in power. He became famous for being a destiny risk-taker for God's servants. In wise but covert defiance of the queen's cruel order to target and exterminate all God's servants, Obadiah stuck out his neck to save 100 prophets alive. He hid them in batches of 50s in two caves and fed them with bread and water.

1 Kings 18: 3-6:

3 And Ahab had called Obadia h, who was in charge of his house. (Now Obadiah feared the LORD greatly.

4 For so it was, while Jezebel massacred the prophets of the LORD, that Obadiah had taken one hundred prophets and hidden them, fifty to a cave, and had fed them with bread and water.)

5 And Ahab had said to Obadiah, "Go into the land to all the springs of water and to all the brooks; perhaps we may find grass to keep the horses and mules alive, so that we will not have to kill any livestock.

6 So they divided the land between them to explore it; Ahab went one way by himself, and Obadiah went another way by himself.

For the ministers of God who survived the Jezebel's massacre, Obadiah was a destiny helper who took the risk of saving their lives and preserving their ministries.

5. Destiny Pathfinder

We can humorously call this destiny helper a destiny-GPS (Global Positioning System). He helps you navigate through obstacles and guides you to your success. David suffered the loss of everything he and his loyal soldiers had when the marauding Amalekites army invaded his camp. Even though he had the bravery and God's promise to launch a counter-attack and recover all, he lacked the clue on the direction to go until he found an Egyptian who acted as his destiny GPS.

1 Samuel 30: 11-15:

11 Then they found an Egyptian in the field, and brought him to David; and they gave him bread and he ate, and they let him drink water. (NKJV)

12 And they gave him a piece of a cake of figs and two clusters of raisins. So when he had eaten, his strength came back to him; for he had eaten no bread nor drunk water for three days and three nights.

14 "We made an invasion of the southern area of the Cherethites, in the territory which belongs to Judah, and of the southern area of Caleb; and we burned Ziklag with fire.

15 And David said to him, "Can you take me down to this troop?" So he said, "Swear to me by God that you will neither kill me nor deliver me into the hands of my master, and I will take you down to this troop."

The Egyptian deserter helped David find his way to the invaders, and he made a full recovery in the counter-attack.

A destiny helper could be someone from the camp of the enemies. Never mind!

6. Destiny Way-Maker

Rebekah was a destiny way-maker for her younger son, Jacob. She foresaw death dangling over his head from his brother's threat. Putting the death threat side by side with the promise of Jacob's future dominance, Rebekah saw the threat as existential and a barrier to his glorious future. She quickly arranged for his escape to avoid the obstacle of untimely death.

Genesis 27: 41-44:

41 So Esau hated Jacob because of the blessing with which his father blessed him, and Esau said in his heart, "The days of mourning for my father are at hand; then I will kill my brother Jacob."

42 And the words of Esau her older son were told to Rebekah. So she sent and called Jacob her younger son, and said to him, "Surely your brother Esau comforts himself concerning you by intending to kill you.

43 "Now therefore, my son, obey my voice: arise, flee to my brother Laban in Haran.

> *44 "And stay with him a few days, until your brother's fury turns away,*

By extension, Esau's threat symbolizes the wrath of household adversaries. Some people's worst barrier to destiny fulfillment is their household enemies or local wickedness. A way-making destiny helper will suffice in that case.

7. Destiny Volunteer Fighter

Jonathan's loyalty to David arguably makes him one of the pearls of the entire Bible characters. To say he was a volunteer fighter to help David fulfill his destiny is an understatement. But he was not any less than that if not much more. It takes being a volunteer destiny fighter to put his life on the line for David's safety. Through sheer sentiment, Jonathan should have been on his father's side, Saul. But to him, there comes a time when blood is not thicker than water, especially when the duty to help a destiny beckons.

1 Samuel 20: 1-4:

> *1 Then David fled from Naioth in Ramah, and went and said to Jonathan, "What have I done? What is my iniquity, and what is my sin before your father, that he*

seeks my life?"

2 So Jonathan said to him, "By no means! You shall not die! Indeed, my father will do nothing either great or small without first telling me. And why should my father hide this thing from me? It is not so!"

3 Then David took an oath again, and said, "Your father certainly knows that I have found favor in your eyes, and he has said, 'Do not let Jonathan know this, lest he be grieved.' But truly, as the LORD lives and as your soul lives, there is but a step between me and death."

4 So Jonathan said to David, "Whatever you yourself desire, I will do it for you."

> **A destiny facilitator paves the way for your meeting with those that matter.**

A volunteer destiny fighter can break ranks with his people, family, race, ethnic group, or nationality to help you fulfill your destiny. Jonathan broke ranks with his father, the royal family, and all its benefits to fight for David's destiny fulfillment as though the battle was his.

8. Destiny Endorser

Destiny helpers are not limited to peers, colleagues, or ordinary citizens. Sometimes, they are among individuals occupying the highest positions of authority in governments, businesses, education institutions, or religious bodies. This type of helpers have signatures that open doors, letterhead papers that command attention, business cards that speak volumes, and a network of people and resources that make everything practically possible for them. King Artaxerxes was one of such to Nehemiah's Jerusalem dream project.

Nehemiah 2: 7-9:

7 Furthermore I said to the King, "If it pleases the King, let letters be given to me for the governors of the region beyond the River, that they must permit me to pass through till I come to Judah,

8 "and a letter to Asaph the keeper of the king's forest, that he must give me timber to make beams for the gates of the citadel which pertains to the temple, for the city wall, and for the house that I will occupy." And the King granted them to me according to the good hand of my God upon me.

9 Then I went to the governors in the region beyond the River, and gave them the King's letters. Now the King had sent captains of the army and horsemen with me.

The King gave Nehemiah letters to clear him with the immigration, customs, and border patrol enforcement officers. His majesty gave him another letter authorizing the head of the King's forest guard to supply him with timber for the woodwork part of his proposed project. That was express access to the country's natural resources, particularly in the forest reserve. Added to the official letters given to Nehemiah was the King's provision of a security team led by a Captain to escort him. Artaxerxes used his name, signature, goodwill, and endorsement to help Nehemiah.

9. Destiny Promoter

When Solomon became King, in place of his father David, he literally walked into and inherited his father's massive local and international networks of destiny helpers. Solomon launched his reign by tapping into the existing networks in the armed forces, priesthood, among his father's palace cabinet members, and going as far as David's foreign partners. Hiram, King of Tyre, whose country was rich in cedars, was among his father's foreign partners. Cedars are the unique specie of trees needed for all manna of woodworks and furniture making. Solomon needed them for his proposed temple and house project.

Tapping into the existing network saved him time and resources. His reign hit the ground running through the power and prospects of the networks he tapped into. Hiram became his great destiny promoter by leveraging his previous relationship with David.

1 Kings 5: 1-2, 5-6, 8-9:

1 Now Hiram king of Tyre sent his servants to Solomon, because he heard that they had anointed him King in place of his father, for Hiram had always loved David.

2 Then Solomon sent to Hiram, saying:

5 And behold, I propose to build a house for the name of the LORD my God, as the LORD spoke to my father David, saying, "Your son, whom I will set on your throne in your place, he shall build the house for My name.

6 Now therefore, command that they cut down cedars for me from Lebanon; and my servants will be with your servants, and I will pay you wages for your servants according to whatever you say. For you know there is none among us who has skill to cut timber like the Sidonians.

8 Then Hiram sent to Solomon, saying: I have considered the message which you sent me, and I will do all you desire concerning the cedar and cypress logs.

9 My servants shall bring them down from Lebanon to the sea; I will float them in rafts by sea to the place you indicate to me, and will have them broken apart there; then you can take them away. And you shall fulfill my desire by giving food for my household.

Hiram promoted Solomon's destiny by deploying his men to fill the professional gap nobody in entire Israel could fill. The network yielded both raw materials and skilled expatriate workers to Solomon. In this particular network, Solomon outsourced professionals from Hiram; and in a barter trade deal, Hiram got annual food supplies from him. A network could fail its purpose if you don't give back to it to keep it running. Solomon's network was family-based; yours could be similar or from any other source.

10. Destiny Arbitrator

A destiny arbitrator comes between you and your destiny goal. His work is to make your way smooth. A case study we can cite is Samuel's recovery of the lost donkeys Saul had spent three days searching for without knowing their whereabouts. Their meeting had an underlying divine purpose, but the encounter ended Saul's futile search for the wandering animals. After their meeting and all the rites of kingship that followed, Samuel told him the exact spot to recover the donkeys.

1 Samuel 9: 3-6:

3 Now the donkeys of Kish, Saul's father, were lost. And Kish said to his son Saul, "Please, take one of the servants with you, and arise, go and look for the donkeys."

4 So he passed through the mountains of Ephraim and through the land of Shalisha, but they did not find them. Then they passed through the land of Shaalim, and they were not there. Then he passed through the land of the Benjamites, but they did not find them.

5 When they had come to the land of Zuph, Saul said

to his servant who was with him, "Come, let us return, lest my father cease caring about the donkeys and become worried about us.

6 And he said to him, "Look now, there is in this city a man of God, and he is an honorable man; all that he says surely comes to pass. So let us go there; perhaps he can show us the way that we should go."

1 Samuel 10: 2:

2 "When you have departed from me today, you will find two men by Rachel's tomb in the territory of Benjamin at Zelzah; and they will say to you, 'The donkeys which you went to look for have been found. And now your father has ceased caring about the donkeys and is worrying about you, saying, "What shall I do about my son?"

Destiny arbitrators help make your recovery quick. They save us time; make our paths straight, precise and result-oriented.

11. Destiny Assistant

While a destiny connector links you from the bottom to the top, a destiny assistant holds you up, so you remain at the top. Without the assistance of Aaron and Hur, Moses lifted his hand holding up the rod of victory for the army of Israel in the battle with the Amalekites. As the war prolonged and his hand lowered by degrees, the Israeli military began to lose the fight by degrees. His hand needed to stay steady. Aaron and Hur provided a seat for his comfort and assisted him in holding up his hand until total victory was won.

Exodus 17: 10-13:

10 So Joshua did as Moses said to him, and fought with Amalek. And Moses, Aaron, and Hur went up to the top of the hill.

11 And so it was, when Moses held up his hand, that Israel prevailed; and when he let down his hand, Amalek prevailed.

12 But Moses' hands became heavy; so they took a stone and put it under him, and he sat on it. And Aaron and Hur supported his hands, one on one side, and the other on the other side; and his hands were steady until the going down of the sun.

13 So Joshua defeated Amalek and his people with the edge of the sword.

A destiny assistant may not be responsible for getting you to the top; his job is to help you stay at the top. He prevents you from the typical 'grace-to-grass fall' that bedevils many glorious destinies.

12. Destiny Counselor

Lemuel's mother must have seen kings rise and fall. When her son, Lemuel, became King, she had the proper counsel to guide him with an enthralling opening remark as follows:

Proverbs 31: 1-4:

1 The words of King Lemuel, the utterance which his mother taught him:

2 What, my son? And what, son of my womb? And what, son of my vows?

3 Do not give your strength to women, Nor your ways to that which destroys kings.

4 It is not for kings, O Lemuel, It is not for kings to drink wine, Nor for princes intoxicating drink;

She counseled him against the three principal pitfalls of

great men. I call them the **3 'Ws'** of destiny derailment and death. They are **W**omen (immorality), **W**ine (alcohol), and **W**ealth (materialism). Our children, especially, need to recognize their parents as destiny helpers and take their wise counsels seriously.

In ministry, spiritual children have a lot to learn from spiritual parents. In society, the younger generations have so much to imbibe from the older generations' wisdom, experiences, and counsel. Computers and other technologies don't have all the answers! They cannot replace the wisdom of the sages with anything. Destiny counselors' scars and escapes, mistakes and precisions, successes and failures, frustrations and triumphs, and pains and pleasures will save and guide you.

13. Destiny Help-Initiator

Destiny help-initiators don't wait for you to seek their help. They look at you, identify the areas you need help with, and step in with their resources which could be intellectual, spiritual, financial, material, or otherwise. Jethro was a destiny help-initiator to Moses. In Genesis 18, he went to meet Moses of his own volition and advised Him on how to appoint and delegate elders to attend to the people of Israel. He gave Moses wise counsel. His advice lessened Moses' daily administrative.

Exodus 18: 17-22:

17 So Moses' father-in-law said to him, "The thing that you do is not good.

18 "Both you and these people who are with you will surely wear yourselves out. For this thing is too much for you; you are not able to perform it by yourself.

19 "Listen now to my voice; I will give you counsel, and God will be with you: Stand before God for the people, so that you may bring the difficulties to God.

20 "And you shall teach them the statutes and the laws, and show them the way in which they must walk and the work they must do.

21 "Moreover you shall select from all the people able men, such as fear God, men of truth, hating covetousness; and place such over them to be rulers of thousands, rulers of hundreds, rulers of fifties, and rulers of tens.

> 22 "*And let them judge the people at all times. Then it will be that every great matter they shall bring to you, but every small matter they themselves shall judge. So it will be easier for you, for they will bear the burden with you.*

Moses' father-in-law heard about his ministry fame. He took Moses' wife and two sons to reconcile them with him – he solved Moses' family problem. He advised Moses against breaking down under the burden of his daily work – he solved his health and fitness problems. He recommended that Moses teach the people generally and attend only to peculiar problems – he solved methodology problems in his ministry. Jethro counseled him to raise, train, and delegate leaders to support him on the job – he solved leadership and administrative problem in his calling.

The problems Jethro's counsel solved in Moses' marriage, life and ministry quantify the help he rendered to his destiny. Jethro took the initiative to provide all the services Moses enjoyed. He remains a classic example of a destiny help-initiator. People like this look at you and voluntarily fix what you lack.

14. Destiny Collaborator

In this category are people known as partners. They

find areas of collaboration to move your destiny forward. Paul found business and ministry collaboration with Aquila and Priscilla. They could stay together without friction or without one party becoming a burden to the other. A destiny collaborator is never a burden but a burden sharer.

Acts 18: 2-3

2 And he found a certain Jew named Aquila, born in Pontus, who had recently come from Italy with his wife Priscilla (because Claudius had commanded all the Jews to depart from Rome); and he came to them.

3 So, because he was of the same trade, he stayed with them and worked; for by occupation they were tentmakers.

A common ground, interest, or goal attracts a destiny collaborator to your life. Destiny collaboration is a symbiotic relationship that benefits both parties. In the absence of that, any resulting collaboration is by force, pretentious and parasitic.

15. Destiny Lifter

A destiny lifter lifts you when you are down. Joseph

lifted the hope, spirit, and life of the butler in prison. The exhortations, motivations, and insightful words that fire you up and re-invigorate you to rise from a fall should not be taken for granted. They come from a destiny helper against the wishes of others who want to keep you down with their words.

Genesis 40: 6-7, 12-13:

6 And Joseph came in to them in the morning and looked at them, and saw that they were sad.

7 So he asked Pharaoh's officers who were with him in the custody of his lord's house, saying, "Why do you look so sad today?"

12 And Joseph said to him, "This is the interpretation of it: The three branches are three days.

13 "Now within three days Pharaoh will lift up your head and restore you to your place, and you will put Pharaoh's cup in his hand according to the former manner, when you were his butler.

Some people truncated their destinies through suicide for lack of destiny lifters when their spirits went down. The journey to depression can be prevented when a destiny lifter stands in your way and makes you believe that 'you can; don't quit.'

16. Destiny Mentor

Mentorship is available in any field. In ministry, Paul mentored Timothy, Elijah mentored Elisha, Rev. Josiah Olufemi Akindayomi, the Founder of the Redeemed Christian Church Of God RCCG), mentored Daddy E. A Adeboye, the present General Overseer of the church worldwide, and Christ mentored the twelve Apostles.

Destiny helpers mentor you, advise you and give you feedback when they feel you are going in directions that you ought not to go. Former President, Barack Obama, said the late Senator John McCain played the role of checks and balances in his life in the White House. Everyone needs a check to apply caution, an urge to keep moving, and an example to follow. That's what a mentor does.

1 Timothy 4: 14:

Do not neglect the gift that is in you, which was given to you by prophecy with the laying on of the hands of the eldership.

A mentor helps you to discover your gifts and motivates you to develop and deploy them. He presents himself as an example you can reliably follow.

17. Destiny Supporter

A destiny supporter lends a helping hand. He may be unable to carry the entire load, but his support is enough to give you the balance you need. Destinies tilt, trip, and flip when they lack support. A destiny supporter is a shoulder to lean on. Every destiny needs three essential supports: prayer support, financial support, and professional support.

Destiny Giver

Everybody gives at different levels. Those raised to give in support of your destiny are far more liberal in giving. They can give everything they have to provide everything you need. Peter gave his only boat to Jesus, the widow of Zarephath gave her only, and last meal to Elijah, and Abigail gave to David what her husband wanted to greedily horde to his own hurt.

1 Samuel 25: 18-24:

18 Then Abigail made haste and took two hundred

loaves of bread, two skins of wine, five sheep already dressed, five seahs of roasted grain, one hundred clusters of raisins, and two hundred cakes of figs, and loaded them on donkeys.

19 And she said to her servants, "Go on before me; see, I am coming after you." But she did not tell her husband Nabal.

20 So it was, as she rode on the donkey, that she went down under cover of the hill; and there were David and his men, coming down toward her, and she met them.

21 Now David had said, "Surely in vain I have protected all that this fellow has in the wilderness, so that nothing was missed of all that belongs to him. And he has repaid me evil for good.

22 "May God do so, and more also, to the enemies of David, if I leave one male of all who belong to him by morning light."

23 Now when Abigail saw David, she hastened to dismount from the donkey, fell on her face before David, and bowed down to the ground.

24 So she fell at his feet and said: "On me, my lord, on

me let this iniquity be! And please let your maidservant speak in your ears, and hear the words of your maidservant.

A destiny giver will sacrifice anything and, if necessary, everything to give in support of a destiny. People like this don't wait for convenience to do what must be done.

To summarize the points, a destiny helper is a divine tool defined as follows:

- ✓ Someone designed and programmed by God to move you to your next level.

- ✓ A catalyst to your destiny fulfillment. A catalyst is a substance that speeds up a chemical reaction. A destiny catalyst catalyzes or speeds you up to your destiny fulfillment.

- ✓ The person prepared by heaven to provide the help you need to achieve your goals in life

- ✓ A person that plays a defining role in your life at a defining period

- ✓ The man or woman to give you divine direction in life.

It is a tragedy to miss destiny helpers. Anyone who misses their destiny helpers has forfeited their purpose for living. Our destiny answers to our purpose in the world.

2

Any Destiny Helper Is God's Tool

According to anthropologists, the evolution of tools runs parallel to human history. Human societies grow and develop proportionally to their available tools. From old-fashioned prehistoric tools to modern manual and electrically-powered tools, today's world has witnessed a revolution in tools invention and usage. Jobs are easier and better done with the right tools. Moreover, the right tools in the right hands produce the right results.

God's infinite creativity makes Him the Master of all in the art of creating, building, and classifying tools for different assignments. He has unimaginable resources of visible and invisible tools. These tools range from living to non-living things and from terrestrial to celestial bodies. His tools storage holds the widest variety of tools. He never has a shortage of tools to get His job done.

Human beings labeled *'Destiny Helpers'* are in one of God's toolboxes. They are His special tools used to fix destinies. They are the people He uses to accomplish His plans and purposes in the lives of others. Destiny helpers connect directly to human destinies. Their primary engagement in fixing human destinies makes them unique among God's general tools.

Anytime God deploys them, a destiny receives help, safeguard, or assistance. You can tell that a vehicle tyre is about to be fixed when the owner brings out a wheel spanner or a drill and a trolley jack, bottle jack, or scissor jack. The tools reveal the work to be done and the user's intention. Destinies receive phenomenal boosts to bloom in the season God releases destiny helpers.

❖ Prayerlessness Causes Destiny's Helplessness

> *Human beings labeled 'Destiny Helpers' are in one of God's toolboxes. They are His special tools used to fix destinies.*

Asking God to send destiny helpers to our individual lives should be part of our daily prayers. The prayer aligns with Christ's teaching on Kingdom Harvest Management (KHV) principle. As the world is ripe for harvest into God's Kingdom, many destinies are also ripe for manifestation and fulfillment. In both cases, our duty is to pray that the Lord of the harvest would send laborers into His work. While the soul-winning field needs the soul winners' labor, the destiny fulfillment field needs destiny helpers' assistance.

The text excerpted below contains the KHM principles:

Matthew 9: 35-38:

35 Then Jesus went about all the cities and villages, teaching in their synagogues, preaching the gospel of the kingdom, and healing every sickness and every disease among the people.

36 But when He saw the multitudes, He was moved with compassion for them, because they were weary and scattered, like sheep having no shepherd.

36 But when He saw the multitudes, He was moved with compassion for them, because they were weary and scattered, like sheep having no shepherd.

37 Then He said to His disciples, "The harvest truly is plentiful, but the laborers are few.

38 "Therefore pray the Lord of the harvest to send out laborers into His harvest."

The general presumption that God will send destinies helpers without praying is erroneous. Jesus saw the need for the harvest and the urgency of laborers' deployment. He saw the risks of a huge loss if laborers did not take prompt action to harvest the ripe fruits. Nevertheless, He implied that prayer is the first action we need to prompt heaven's deployment of laborers.

From Jesus' teaching on souls' harvest, one would assume that the Lord of the harvest shouldn't wait for us to pray before sending the workforce into His business of soul-winning. The assumption is wrong because God follows the rules of our engagement in doing His work. One of the rules states that '*For we are labourers together with God: ye are God's husbandry, ye are God's building.*' 1 Corinthians 3: 6 (KJV). We are in a partnership deal with God in the business of our destiny fulfillment.

Every aspect of God's work we are called to do is on a partnership deal with Him. We can't do it alone even if we wish to, and He won't do it alone even though He can. God's work includes destiny fulfillment. He wants to see people live and maximize the life He designed for them. Many destinies will fail if we are not conscious and committed to the partnership deal in destiny fulfillment. Therefore, our duty is to pray for the designer of destinies to raise and release destiny helpers for our destiny fulfillment.

I like how the Lord's words connect in verse 38 to reinforce the message. By beginning with 'therefore,' the Lord drew a logical conclusion. Since the logical conclusion about our destiny fulfillment is that we need destiny helpers as God's tools in our lives, not praying to have them is illogical. In the same verse, the Lord connects the word '*pray*' with '*send,*' implying

The general presumption that God will send destinies helpers without praying is erroneous.

that God will send destiny helpers to us only in response to prayer. You may have been denying yourself destiny helpers' services by delaying prayer on the subject.

If you want God to send the destiny helpers you need, take action in prayer. Consider payer as a logical conclusion at the present crossroads on the road to your destiny fulfillment. In Philippians 4: 6, prayer is like an official request forwarded to the company management. The text says, '*Be anxious for nothing, but in everything by prayer and supplication, with thanksgiving, let your requests be made known to God.*' In everything that pertains to your destiny fulfillment, create no room for worries or anxieties. Send your petitions to God through prayers and wait for His response.

❖ Two Categories Of Destiny Helpers

Anything in creation is a potential tool in God's hands.

However, I want to narrow down destiny helpers to two categories of humans as God's tools. All the eighteen types of destiny helpers I enumerated in the previous chapter fall into either of the two categories.

The first category comprises unbelievers who vary in ranks of ungodliness. When God wants to use them, their ungodliness does not matter. In His sovereignty, He bends them to get His job done. You can call them unwilling tools in God's hands. Their unwillingness does not matter when God employs them as tools for His tasks. A typical example is that God used a heathen king called Cyrus to liberate His people and facilitate reformation in Israel.

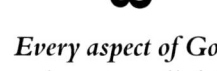

Every aspect of God's work we are called to do is on a partnership deal with Him.

Isaiah 45: 1-5:

1. "Thus says the LORD to His anointed, To Cyrus, whose right hand I have held-To subdue nations before him And loose the armor of kings, To open before him the double doors, So that the gates will not be shut:

2 'I will go before you And make the crooked places straight; I will break in pieces the gates of bronze And cut the bars of iron.

3 I will give you the treasures of darkness And hidden riches of secret places, That you may know that I, the LORD, Who call you by your name, Am the God of Israel.

4 For Jacob My servant's sake, And Israel My elect, I have even called you by your name; I have named you, though you have not known Me.

5 I am the LORD, and there is no other; There is no God besides Me. I will gird you, though you have not known Me,

The text reveals how God uses unbelievers as tools to accomplish destiny fulfillment for an individual or a group of persons. We can sum it as follows:

- ✓ **God's Spirit Influences Unbelievers To Help Destinies**

In exercising His authority over creation, God engaged the services of an unbelieving ruler to initiate the freedom of His people. The man's name was Cyrus the Great, a king of an ancient kingdom. After he conquered Babylon, God prompted him to decree that the Jews should rebuild the Jerusalem temple.

We can call Cyrus' decree the Foreign Affairs or Foreign Mission of his empire. From Babylon to Jerusalem, on a straight course, was slightly above 1678 miles which would take over 24 hours to drive at the average speed of 65 miles per hour. It couldn't have been anything less than the influence of God's Spirit upon this great ruler to proclaim a religious reform and freedom in Jerusalem. God can influence unbelievers to formulate and pursue policies to suit the destinies of His people.

> *When God holds up the hands of our destiny helpers, they have no choice but to hold up our hands.*

The second thing Cyrus did under the influence of God's Spirit was that he relaxed the immigration policies of Babylon to enable the Jews willing to travel to Jerusalem to do so. We can refer to this move as Amnesty for the captive Jews. It makes us understand that God can influence or prompt anybody in the position of power to make policy changes on immigration, freedom of movement, religious freedom, and reformation to suit His people.

God called Cyrus His '*anointed.*' As the text uses it, the word means a divine messenger, tool, instrument, or vessel. Cyrus was not anointed with the Holy Spirit because of his faith or purity. He was brought under the influence of the Holy Spirit as a tool to fix destinies and, as such, became the Lord's anointed.

✓ God Holds Unbelievers' Hands To Help Destinies

God's word about Cyrus creates a picture of a helpless man in God's grips so that he might help God's people. Who can wriggle out of the hands of the Almighty? God described Cyrus as a tool, a destiny helper *'whose right hand I have held.'* When God holds up the hands of our destiny helpers, they have no choice but to hold up our hands.

Under the influence of the Holy Spirit, a heathen became a willing tool in God's hands. Such is the mystery of God's sovereignty and the greatness of His power and wisdom to perform any task. Having the Spirit upon him was complemented with God holding Cyrus' right hand as the Scripture says.

3

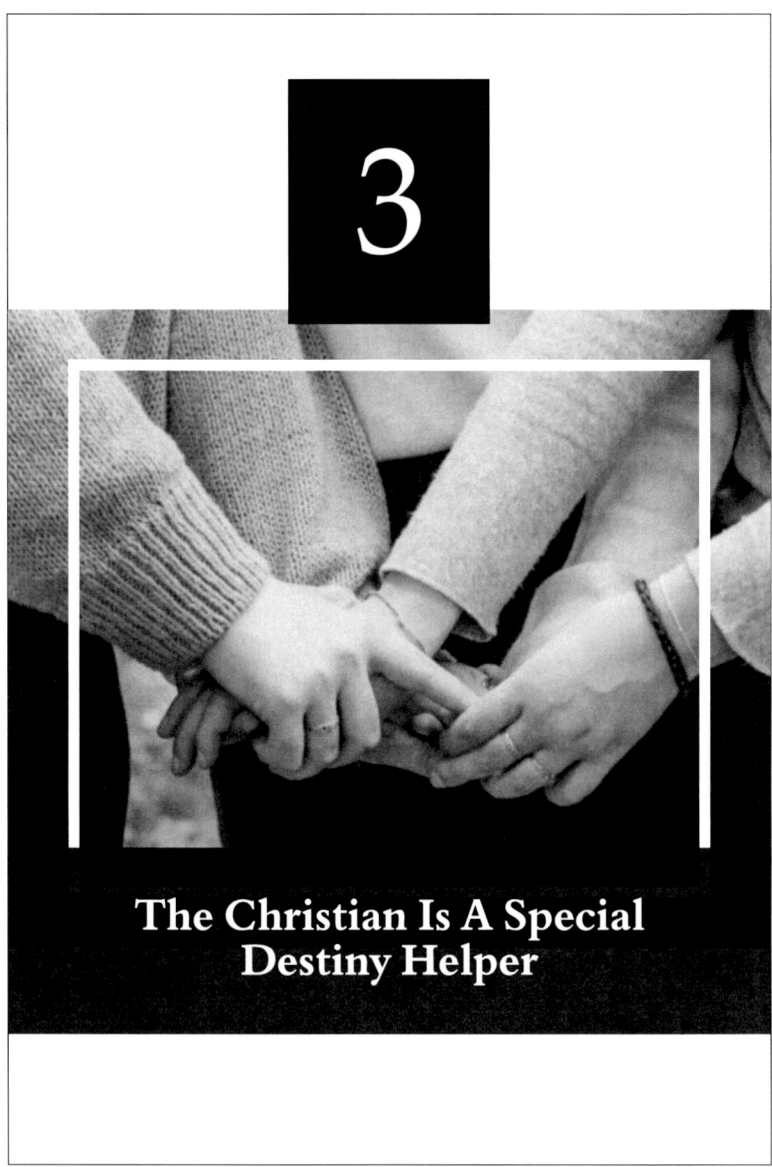

The Christian Is A Special Destiny Helper

The inspired writing in the book of Ephesians calls the second category of human tools in God's hands' *His workmanship.*' These are special tools because they belong to God by right of redemption and benefits of a relationship. They are more receptive and responsive to carrying out God's commissions. Every believer in Christ belongs to this class.

By God's design, believers in Christ are primarily the tools for divine tasks on earth. It tells you how much fail when believers fail. Besides, it suggests how many destinies depend on the believers' response and surrender to God's usage. Every child of God occupies a significant space in God's toolbox of fixing human destinies.

Ephesians 2: 10:

For we are His workmanship, created in Christ Jesus for good works, which God prepared beforehand that we should walk in them.

Two things are attached to the believers' life as God's tools. We are created in Christ for a purpose that the Bible defines as '*good works.*' Secondly, we are '*prepared beforehand*' or programmed for good works. Believers who fail to function as programmed are malfunctioning. And so is a church – the collective body of Christ in any location – which fails to function as programmed.

> *By God's design, believers in Christ are primarily the tools for divine tasks on earth.*

A malfunctioning believer cannot fix human destinies any more than a malfunctioning tool can fix a task. How well you function as God has programmed you is how useful you are in God's business of fixing destinies.

In a general sense, every human is God's invention as a tool. But the fact that the natural human volition often obstructs His usage of humans as tools, God re-invented a new generation of people with transformed volitions. This fact makes everyone in Christ primarily a destiny helper. And like a tool among other tools in a toolbox, everyone in the body of Christ shouldn't lack destiny helpers. Fellow tools surround us in God's toolbox.

As the word '*destiny*' runs throughout the content of this book, there is a need to define it for a more precise understanding and contextual use. I would like to draw the definition of destiny from God's word in Isaiah, which says:

Isaiah 43: 7:

Everyone who is called by My name, Whom I have created for My glory; I have formed him, yes, I have made him."

From the above Biblical text, we can define destiny as God's glory designed to manifest in each person's life. If we re-arrange the text, we will have this '*Everyone …is…created for My glory….*' In other words, God created everyone to manifest a certain kind of His glory at different levels and intensities.

Everything God puts in everyone – gifts, talents, potentials, anointing, abilities, and others – is to promote His glory. In whatever area we function, our destiny is to manifest and advance God's glory. How does God reveal and advertise His glory in human lives? He does that in various ways.

✓ **Manifesting Special Academic Abilities**

God manifested special learning abilities in Daniel, Shadrach, Meshach, and Abednego in the Babylonian

Academy. He promoted His glory as the giver of good gifts and rare skills in a proportion no power on earth can match. The four students outsmarted their colleagues by an Intelligence Quotient (IQ) rated ten times higher than the highest among their colleagues. They were found better than the best, which was found in Babylon's best and most competitive Academy.

Daniel 1: 19-20:

19. Then the king interviewed them, and among them all none was found like Daniel, Hananiah, Mishael, and Azariah; therefore they served before the king.

20. And in all matters of wisdom and understanding about which the king examined them, he found them ten times better than all the magicians and astrologers who were in all his realm.

✓ Manifesting Special Wisdom

He manifested unique wisdom in Daniel to unravel mysteries. He advertised His glory as the revealer of secrets and the giver of the insight to solve all puzzles.

Daniel 2: 17-18:

27 Daniel answered in the presence of the king, and said, "The secret which the king has demanded, the wise men, the astrologers, the magicians, and the soothsayers cannot declare to the king.

28 "But there is a God in heaven who reveals secrets, and He has made known to King Nebuchadnezzar what will be in the latter days. Your dream, and the visions of your head upon your bed, were these:

✓ Manifesting Special Supernatural Power

At the palace of Pharaoh in ancient Egypt, He revealed His supreme power through Moses and advertised His glory as the unbeatable Almighty God. Pharaoh's sponsored challengers, which included the Egyptian wise men and the sorcerers, acknowledged that the supreme power Moses demonstrated could only be the *finger of God* at work.

Exodus 7: 10-12:

10 So Moses and Aaron went in to Pharaoh, and they did so, just as the LORD commanded. And Aaron cast down his rod before Pharaoh and before his servants, and it became a serpent.

11 But Pharaoh also called the wise men and the sorcerers; so the magicians of Egypt, they also did in like manner with their enchantments.

12 For every man threw down his rod, and they became serpents. But Aaron's rod swallowed up their rods.

Exodus 8: 18-19:

18 Now the magicians so worked with their enchantments to bring forth lice, but they could not. So there were lice on man and beast.

19 Then the magicians said to Pharaoh, "This is the finger of God." But Pharaoh's heart grew hard, and he did not heed them, just as the LORD had said.

- ✓ **Manifesting His Holiness**

We can cite many more examples of how God reveals and promotes His glory in the Bible. By giving moral laws to Israel, He set them apart as His holy people. Hence, God revealed and promoted His glory through their holiness as the Holy One among idol-worshipping nations.

Leviticus 19: 1-2:

1 And the LORD spoke to Moses, saying,

2 "Speak to all the congregation of the children of Israel, and say to them: 'You shall be holy, for I the LORD your God am holy.

✓ Manifesting Special Creative Talents

In whatever area we function, our destiny is to manifest and advance God's glory.

During the tabernacle building in the wilderness, He manifested exceptional creativity in Bezaleel and his colleagues. He promoted His glory as the source of creative arts and all creative works in any field.

Exodus 36: 1-2:

1 "And Bezalel and Aholiab, and every gifted artisan in whom the LORD has put wisdom and understanding, to know how to do all manner of work for the service of the sanctuary, shall do according to all that the LORD has commanded."

2 Then Moses called Bezalel and Aholiab, and every gifted artisan in whose heart the LORD had put wisdom, everyone whose heart was stirred, to come and do the work.

✓ Manifesting Special Administrative Wisdom

Solomon's wisdom in evolving economic and political systems the like of which the world had never seen before pointed all curious hearts to God, the giver. His unusual insight into complicated matters and his flawless procedures in resolving civil crises among the Jews compelled men and women across the country and in the international circle to glorify God on his behalf.

> *How well you function as God has programmed you is how useful you are in God's business of fixing destinies.*

1 Kings 4: 29-30:

29 And God gave Solomon wisdom and exceedingly great understanding, and largeness of heart like the sand on the seashore.

30 Thus Solomon's wisdom excelled the wisdom of all the men of the East and all the wisdom of Egypt.

Any position God puts us in, and whatever He wants us to do with His resources in our lives is our destiny. We can't manifest His glory if we miss His mandate. Our destiny connects directly with what He wants us to do.

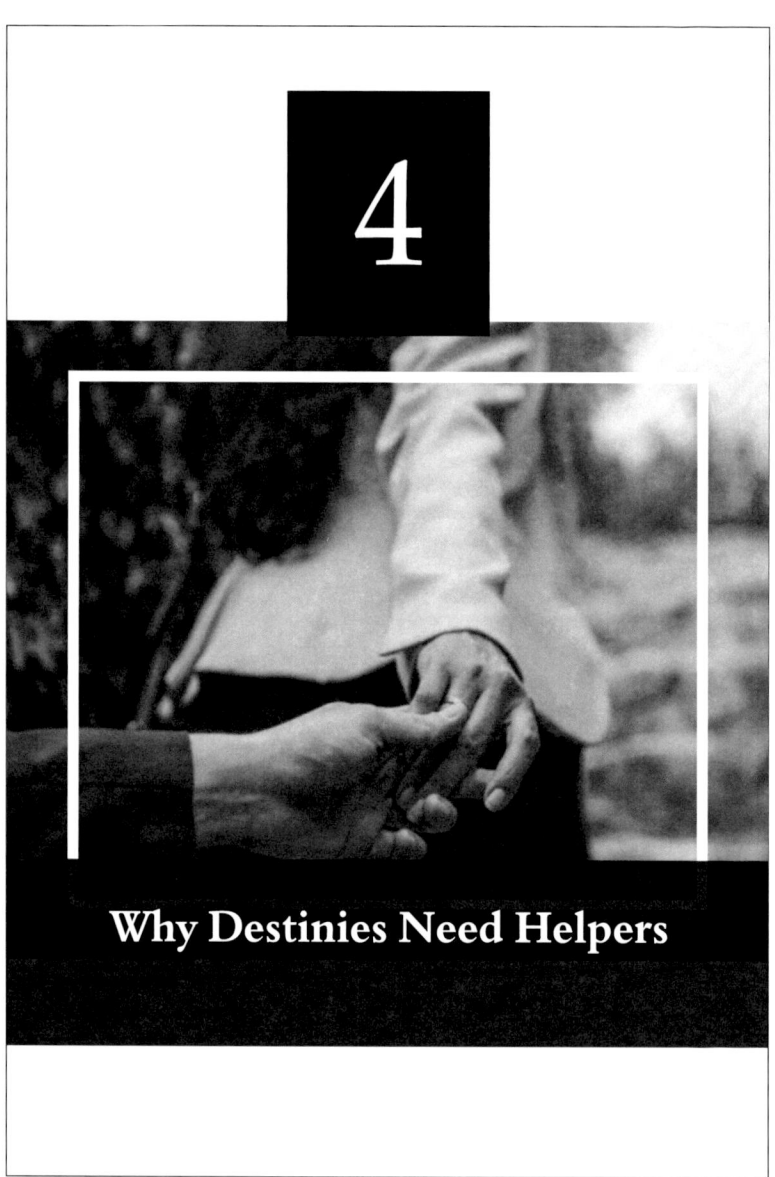

4

Why Destinies Need Helpers

Every destiny has its place and time in the world. Along with its evil forces, the world is the first enemy of destinies. It is the place where destinies survive or are strangled. The world is the stage where destinies shine or are eclipsed. The main reason destinies need help is that they are designed to shine in the world. But the world and its forces don't naturally support destiny survival and fulfillment.

The man called Job was one of the world's earliest philosophers who made many astute philosophical statements recorded in the Bible. Many Christians look at him as a prominent Bible character of unusual uprightness in a narrow sense. Beyond the records of his distinguished godliness, strong faith in God, and patience in trials, his insight ranks with that of Solomon and other Bible characters. Their words qualify as the world's earliest, truest and timeless philosophies.

Now let's listen to Job on the fate of destinies in the global environment called 'the world.' Job 5: 6-7 says, 'For affliction does not come from the dust, Nor does trouble spring from the ground; 7. Yet man is born to trouble, As the sparks fly upward.' Job says every destiny is born into a world of troubles. His statement is a timeless submission about births, purposes, destinies, survivals, and fatality. Every destiny needs help because the world is a battlefield, a place of many afflictions, and a territory of numerous troubles.

Animal behavior and responses to the changes in their environment explain the relationship between destiny survival and the troubles in the world. The grassland provides food, shelter, and camouflage for the young deer in the rainy season. In the dry season, the same grassland exposes the young deer to danger and forces it to migrate for survival. With less grass around, its camouflage, shelter, and food are threatened.

The world changes in rhythm with different forces. Seasons of war and peace and eras of problems and prospects keep every destiny in a circle where survival becomes a deliberate act. In John 16: 33, Jesus emphatically says "'These things I have spoken to you, that in Me you may have peace. In the world you will have tribulation; but be of good cheer, I have overcome the world." In the world, tribulations confront every destiny. In this context, Jesus describes Himself as an alternative habitation where the peace that ensures destiny fulfillment is a reality.

The same world in which we want our destinies to shine and be fulfilled is the same place that poses the worst dangers to our destinies' survival. Troubles in the world affect destinies in different ways. The fact that they exist in this hostile world makes every destiny in need of help to survive and shine. Good enough, God has made us helps in each other's life.

While you are praying to God to send you destiny helpers, remember you are destiny helper to some people. Do what you can do for others, and let others do what you can't do for yourself. I call it the first rule of survival and success, which subscribes to the golden rule of "'And just as you want men to do to you, you also do to them likewise.' Luke 6: 31.

> *Every destiny has its place and time in the world.*

Like anything else in the world, a destiny can encounter problems. The reality of problems in the path of destiny fulfillment is why destinies need helpers. Some of the problems destinies face and why they need help include the fact that:

✓ **A Destiny Can Be Truncated**

Samson's destiny was truncated through his marriage. After two failed marriage attempts, he eventually met Delilah and proposed marriage to her. Samson was on a mission to marry a woman he loved, but Delilah was on a mission to betray the man of unusual strength to the Philistines. The Philistines were her countrymen who had declared Samson as their most wanted enemy.

Delilah fixed her eyes on the bounties placed on Samson's head while Samson focused his attention on the beauty nature bestowed upon her. At the foundation of this marriage were two conflicting interests of the spouses-to-be.

For Samson, his destiny helpers were his parents, who volunteered sound counsel to guide him right, but he ignored them and despised their counsel. His passion for Delilah pushed him down the hill; he never stopped tumbling until he lay dead with the Philistines. His destiny to destroy the philistines and stay alive to enjoy the victory with the Israelites was truncated.

Judges 14: 1- 3:

1 Now Samson went down to Timnah, and saw a woman in Timnah of the daughters of the Philistines.

2 So he went up and told his father and mother, saying, "I have seen a woman in Timnah of the daughters of the Philistines; now therefore, get her for me as a wife."

3 Then his father and mother said to him, "Is there no woman among the daughters of your brethren, or among all my people, that you must go and get a wife from the uncircumcised Philistines?" And Samson said to his father, "Get her for me, for she pleases me well."

The possibility of a destiny being truncated makes the role of a destiny helper a necessity. Many great destinies have suffered a similar fate as Samson's through taking wrong or miscalculated steps in marriage. Delilah symbolizes a marriage partner with a painful mission; an enemy pretending to be a friend; a spy pretending to be an ally; a betrayer pretending to be a loyalist; and a pretentious lover pretending to be genuine.

> *Every destiny needs help because the world is a battlefield, a place of many afflictions, and a territory of numerous troubles.*

Judges 14: 4 says, '*4 But his father and mother did not know that it was of the LORD-that He was seeking an occasion to move against the Philistines. For at that time the Philistines had dominion over Israel.*' The text makes some Bible scholars conclude that Samson's doomed marriage was inevitable and his rejection of his destiny helpers' counsel was justifiable.

I tend to look at the context from a broader perspective. God was seeking an occasion to make Israel or an Israelite the aggressor of the Philistines. The Philistines had been the provocateurs of Israel all along. If it was God's design for Samson to marry a Philistine lady, must she be Delilah? If it must, must Samson reveal the secret of his supernatural strength? Shouldn't the parents' counsel have been a guideline, even though it generalized and wrote off all the Philistine ladies?

If God wants you to marry from a nationality, tribe, ethnic group, church, ministry, or place, the counsel of a destiny helper can help you make the right choice. For instance, God's word denounces the concept of the unequal yoke with unbelievers as 2 Corinthians 6: 14 says, '*14 Do not be unequally yoked together with unbelievers. For what fellowship has righteousness with lawlessness? And what communion has light with darkness?*'

Trying to marry a child of God or a fellow believer in Christ does not make every child of God or every believer in Christ, the right partner for you. A destiny helper's counsel will narrow your choice from God's generally approved people to a specifically authorized choice.

✓ Destiny Can Be Exchanged

To illustrate this phenomenon, the Biblical story of the two women who argued about the ownership of a living and a dead child captures the concept. By the way, the idea of exchange is about '*give and take.*' The 'give and take' nature of exchange makes it appear harmless until the items exchanged are weighed on the value scale. A destiny that suffers an exchange still has something, but it is something inferior to what is lost. No same human wants to trade something valuable for a worthless thing.

> *In the world, tribulations confront every destiny.*

The full text of the story is found in 1 Kings 3: 16-28. But the part of it which illustrates the possibility and consequence of destiny exchange is stated below:

1 Kings 3: 16-22:

16 Now two women who were harlots came to the king, and stood before him.

17 And one woman said, "O my lord, this woman and I dwell in the same house; and I gave birth while she was in the house.

18 "Then it happened, the third day after I had given birth, that this woman also gave birth. And we were together; no one was with us in the house, except the two of us in the house.

19 "And this woman's son died in the night, because she lay on him.

20 "So she arose in the middle of the night and took my son from my side, while your maidservant slept, and laid him in her bosom, and laid her dead child in my bosom.

21 "And when I rose in the morning to nurse my son, there he was, dead. But when I had examined him in the morning, indeed, he was not my son whom I had borne."

22 Then the other woman said, "No! But the living one is my son, and the dead one is your son." And the first woman said, "No! But the dead one is your son, and the living one is my son." Thus they spoke before the king.

Both women still had a child, but one argued that the

living child was hers and the other countered that the dead child wasn't hers either. One of them accidentally suffocated her baby in the night. When she woke to discover that the baby was dead, she quietly and cleverly picked up the living child from her friend's bed and replaced him with the dead child, covered with the same clothes. In other words, she exchanged the dead with the living child.

As the dead child's mother did the wicked exchange '*in the middle of the night,*' forces of darkness and their agents strike in the middle of the night. Among many evils they perpetrate is the evil exchange of destinies. The Bible says '*Another parable He put forth to them, saying: "The kingdom of heaven is like a man who sowed good seed in his field; 25 "but while men slept, his enemy came and sowed tares among the wheat and went his way.*' Matthew 13: 24-25. A state of spiritual sleep can open the door for the operation of an evil exchange.

The mother of the living child had a dead child after the exchange. Of what value is the dead to a living child? When destiny exchange takes place, whatever the enemy uses to replace whatever he takes is of no importance. Anything you receive in exchange for what you give away as far as your destiny is concerned is worthless. Your destiny is all the value by which your life is estimated.

Waking up in the morning, the woman with the living child burst into an argument with her friend. She had been shortchanged overnight. The argument raged on until Solomon intervened to resolve it. A continuous state of argument within yourself or with people about your true identity, potential, or capability may signal that an evil exchange has taken place in your life. Something keeps telling you within that, 'This is not whom you are meant to be. You could do better than this. This is not where God intends to take you.' Arguments over ownership, identity, and possession can be a red light of an exchanged destiny.

Solomon's wise counsel revealed the true owner of the living child, and his royal order reversed the exchange. A destiny helper with an unusual insight into mysteries would help throw light on the problem of exchanged destiny. Most importantly, a decree or prayer to reverse the exchange is the final action to complete the restoration process.

A destiny can suffer delay or derailment. It can be cursed or corrupted. Destiny can be set back or stagnated. Destiny can

A destiny can suffer delay or derailment.

be weak or wasted. Destiny can be stolen; it can be covered to prevent its glory from shining. Destiny can be cast down from its lofty height and trampled under men's feet. A destiny can suffer enslavement; it can be oppressed, afflicted, or distorted.

God's tools are used to solve problems. By extension, destiny helpers are God's tools used to solve destiny problems.

5

When God Uses A Destiny Helper

What happens when God uses a destiny helper for us? Before I summarize our gains when God uses a destiny helper, let me share a story. A woman wanted to join her husband, who won a scholarship to study in the United States of America. By law, she was entitled to join her husband because it was a foreign scholarship. Anytime she went to the embassy, she was denied a visa. After each denial, she repeatedly applied eighteen times, and the embassy kept denying her on each occasion.

She was alone in Nigeria, a newlywed without a child yet. It was a lonesome experience. Then she was invited to a meeting where they raised prayers for destiny helpers. She reapplied for the visa at the same embassy, which denied her application eighteen times. The interviewer asked a simple question: 'Why do you want to go to America?' At the end of it all, she got the visa.

There are many benefits we derive from the encounter with destiny helpers God positions in our way.

The interviewer who reviewed her application with the same question she had answered eighteen times before was her destiny helper. Nothing changes in anyone's life until a destiny helper is encountered. With a destiny helper at work in your life, you will get a 'yes' where you got a 'no' before. There are many benefits we derive from the encounter with destiny helpers God positions in our way. Some of the benefits are:

✓ We Go Faster In Life

Paul's mandate received accelerated preparation and integration into the existing apostolic network in Jerusalem through Barnabas, who aided his introduction and acceptance among them.

✓ We Make A Quicker Recovery

We recover quicker from wastage. The Egyptian David encountered on his recovery mission aided his speedy recovery of what he lost.

✓ We Dare To Dream Big

We attempt great things for God. Nathan was David's destiny helper who always gave him supernatural insight and inspired words from the Lord. He was a light in David's path. David's attempt to embark on the great temple project must have been due to his confidence in Nathan's counsel.

between you and the people that God has strategically positioned to assist you in realizing your dreams. There are some people somewhere that God has arranged to catapult you to your next level - they are called destiny helpers.

Prayers:

1) I pray that the power blocking your destiny helper shall be paralyzed, in Jesus' mighty name.

2) Any power stopping your destiny helpers shall be stopped, in Jesus' mighty name.

3) Any fake power occupying the seat of your destiny helpers shall be unseated by fire, in the name of Jesus.

4) Every form of carefully designed blindness to make you miss your destiny helpers shall be wiped away by the blood of Jesus, in Jesus' mighty name.

5) Pray for yourself and say, 'Father, make me a destiny helper, in Jesus' name.'

6

When A Destiny Helper Is Under Attack

A destiny helper is a divinely arranged alliance for success. Without a helper, a destiny stands alone. It is vulnerable and more likely to fail than succeed in that state. Weakening an existing alliance or preventing a new one from being formed is one of the enemy's strategies to waste destinies. An attack against your destiny helper is an indirect attack against you.

A man was scheduled for a job interview in an oil company. Seeking employment in the oil and gas industry was (and is still) every job applicant's dream. The salary scale is usually mouthwatering, and the benefits remain attractive and incredible. His friend's father was the company's Deputy Managing Director (MD). For that reason, the interview was considered a foregone conclusion. He only needed to fulfill the formality of being available to satisfy the employment requirements.

The first applicant on the list of shortlisted candidates was called in for the interview. Time ticked away by the seconds and minutes. Soon, the second interviewee was called in. The man introduced to his friend's father, the deputy MD, was the third to be called in. As he was about to enter the interview room, the deputy MD had a cramp. He rushed to use the bathroom but had no relief. While the interview session was to run for this special applicant, he was frequenting the bathroom to ease up.

Meanwhile, other interview panel members had to continue the interview without the deputy MD who was supposed to ease the applicant's interview. Unfortunately for the applicant, he was not prepared for the interview like others who had nobody to influence the interview outcome on the panel.

The deputy MD was to use his position and power to waive the interview process for his smooth passage. He was unprepared yet facing a panel of interviewers he was not familiar with. Their job was to interview him objectively and fairly, as they did for the first two applicants.

> *Any attack on destiny helpers affects the beneficiaries of the help.*

They asked him the first question. He was caught off guard and couldn't answer because he was unprepared for it. Fidgeting and jittery, the interviewers saw the air of apprehension and unpreparedness around him. They asked him a difficult question which felt like a jab. He was confused the more. Even when they asked him, 'What is your name?' he could not tell them. It was so embarrassing. The enemy relocated his destiny helper before he was called to face the interview.

His story illustrates how a destiny helper can come under the devil's attack. Any attack on destiny helpers affects the beneficiaries of the help. That's the enemy's goal for attacking a destiny helper. It's an indirect attack strategy of the wicked.

❖ **How Destinies Are Disconnected From Their Helpers**

Michelle Obama used to work as a hostel assistant somewhere. The manager of the hostel didn't like her. She told her, 'I don't like seeing you here, and you even smell.' Then, Michelle was fired. When Obama's wife became the President's wife, the hostel manager applied to her office to be her designer.

She went for the interview, and the First Lady was asked to meet her. 'What's her name?' the First Lady asked, and the name rang a bell in her head when she heard it. She remembered the name and the humiliation, discrimination, embarrassment, and loss of a job that same name meted out to her somewhere in the past. 'The woman that said I smelled,' she recalled.

✓ Loss Of Rare Opportunities

A destiny disconnected from its helpers will suffer the loss of rare opportunities. 'Go tell her, I'm busy. I will not give her my designer's work,' Michelle concluded. The woman would have been great, but her racial bias and maybe personal ego stood against her chances when she met a potential destiny helper. The former hostel manager was disconnected from her destiny helper and lost all the breakthroughs she would have benefited from.

Today's great men and women have destiny helpers somewhere. You should not allow unruly behavior or ungodliness to disconnect you from your destiny helpers. Meeting a destiny helper could occur as casually as meeting anybody else. The only safeguard we have to avoid losing our destiny helpers is to keep a culture of courtesy with everyone everywhere. A simple show of respect could be the key that connects you with your destiny helper.

✓ Loss Of Fame

Disconnecting from a destiny helper makes a destiny crawl into an unknown grave. A destiny could sink into oblivion when it is disconnected from its helper. Take the alliance between Paul and Barnabas as an example. Until they parted ways through irreconcilable differences on an issue relating to their joint ministerial work, Barnabas' name ran copiously across the pages of the Acts of the Apostles.

From the moment they split and went their separate ways, Barnabas' name and ministry sank from the remaining pages of the Bible. The initial fame he enjoyed might have been connected with his alliance with Paul. Silas, who replaced him, enjoyed prominence that Barnabas lost. Paul was the arrowhead of his team's apostolic fame.

A simple show of respect could be the key that connects you with your destiny helper.

Any power trying to chase away your destiny helper shall be buried alive in the name of Jesus.

The enemy evolves strategies to disconnect destinies from their helpers. These strategies vary according to his targets. Their effectiveness is the common feature of all the strategies.

- ✓ **Wrong Alliance**

The connection between Uzziah's reign and Isaiah's rise in ministry almost destroyed Isaiah's assignment. Until Uzziah died, Isaiah was limited in vision, glory, power, and influence in his prophetic ministry. Something about the reign of Uzziah had a negative impact on Isaiah's ministry.

Isaiah 6: 1:

In the year that King Uzziah died, I saw the Lord sitting on a throne, high and lifted up, and the train of His robe filled the temple

As Uzziah died, Isaiah saw the Lord in His glory and majesty. Before Uzziah's death, Isaiah covered five chapters in a ministry that was to span sixty-six chapters of his book.

The enemy evolves strategies to disconnect destinies from their helpers.

- ✓ **Death Of Destiny Helpers**

A more brutal attack of the enemy may lead to a destiny helper's death. Since some families lost their breadwinners, the careers and businesses of many members have been terminated. The breadwinner was their destiny helper.

✓ Replacement Of Destiny Helpers

The Pharaoh, whose dreams Joseph interpreted, was very kind to him and his family. He gave them a parcel of land for their settlement in Egypt. When another Pharaoh replaced him years later, he began to oppress, afflict and enslave the children of Israel.

Exodus 1: 8-11:

8 Now there arose a new king over Egypt, who did not know Joseph.

9 And he said to his people, "Look, the people of the children of Israel are more and mightier than we;

10 "come, let us deal shrewdly with them, lest they multiply, and it happen, in the event of war, that they also join our enemies and fight against us, and so go up out of the land."

11 Therefore they set taskmasters over them to afflict them with their burdens. And they built for Pharaoh supply cities, Pithom and Raamses.

From freedom to bondage, from self-service to forced labor, from emancipation to enslavement, and from independent works to working under stringent supervision, the Israelites suffered a twist of their blessings because the Pharaoh who knew and favored them had died.

7

Right Timing With Destiny Opportunities

It's tragic to miss the time to connect with a destiny helper. Many successful people have acknowledged that being at the right place at the right time was part of their turning point secrets. Had Jesus' disciples not promptly acted when He told them to meet the man with a pitcher of water as they entered the city and followed him, they would have missed their way to where the Passover would be hosted.

Luke 22: 8-13:

8 And He sent Peter and John, saying, "Go and prepare the Passover for us, that we may eat."

9 So they said to Him, "Where do You want us to prepare?"

10 And He said to them, "Behold, when you have entered the city, a man will meet you carrying a pitcher of water; follow him into the house which he enters.

11 "Then you shall say to the master of the house, 'The Teacher says to you, "Where is the guest room where I may eat the Passover with My disciples?"'

12 "Then he will show you a large, furnished upper room; there make ready."

13 So they went and found it just as He had said to them, and they prepared the Passover.

It is a disconnection with a destiny helper when your helper is somewhere, and you're somewhere else. Your helper is in South Africa, and you are in Yugoslavia. Your helper is in Nigeria, but you've been given Visa to go to America. If this is the picture of your life, the enemy has strategized for you to miss your destiny helper.

Alex Fleming was a Scottish scientist famous for discovering the world's first antibiotic known as penicillin. Fleming was a physician and a microbiologist. A story about his educational career says he rescued a wealthy man's son from drowning. As compensation for his kindness, the affluent man asked what he could do for him. Fleming expressed interest in studying medicine, and the wealthy man decided to sponsor his career. Being at a place where he could help someone put him in a position to receive help from someone else. He was at the right place at the right time.

In the second quarter of 2018, international media was agog with the story of a 22-year-old Mamoudou Gassama, an illegal immigrant in France. Providence put him at the right place at the right time when he scaled barriers to the fourth balcony of a high-rise building where a 4-year-old kid was dangling to fall.

His heroic act announced his name across France, Europe, Africa, and the world. He was invited to meet Emmanuel Macron, France's president, and was immediately offered French citizenship and a job in the emergency services. Gassama's attempt to cross the Mediterranean in March 2014 to reach Italy failed because the police caught him until he made the same trip again a year before he illegally crossed into France from Italy.

Mamoudou immediately earned an international reputation as Mali' Spiderman' for no other reason than being at the right place at the right time and seizing the opportunity to do the right thing.

- ✓ **Tragedy Of Diversion**

Diversion from destiny helpers is another strategy the devil uses to attack destinies. A diversion detours you from the path to connect you with your destiny helper. Your attention can also be diverted. You could be with a destiny helper and lose the attention you need to focus on issues that will change your life forever.

In Acts 13: 6-8, a high-ranking public office holder invited Paul to hear the word of eternal life. He wanted to settle the issue of his eternal destiny once and for all. But a sorcerer called Elymas attempted to divert the nobleman's attention from Paul's words. Some people deeply regret meeting their destiny helpers without raising the issues about their destiny. A satanic diversion might have taken them off the subject that would have benefitted them forever.

> *God never intends that we should be stagnant in life.*

✓ Tragedy Of Revenge

When Jesus teaches us to forgive as many times as we are offended, He wants us to leave vengeance to Him. If we don't let go of our hurts and those responsible for them, the result could stand against us in the future.

A Bishop bought a piece of land from an unruly boy. He later found out that the land belonged to eleven people. They went to court and got an injunction that the Bishop should remove his church building from the piece of land. Instead of foreclosing the Bishop's church, they took him to the head of the family to settle the dispute.

On getting to the head of the family, 'Do you remember me, Bishop,' he asked, and the Bishop replied, 'No.' Then the head of the family took him down memory lane and said, 'Years ago, my vehicle hit yours, and your driver dragged me to you. You sat in front of your office. You didn't look at me; all you said was, 'Did anybody die?' and the driver said 'No.'

After that, you said, 'Let the man go.' You didn't know me; you didn't look at me, but you let me go. Bishop, I will give you more land now. The offender whom the Bishop forgave years ago became his destiny helper. That's the power of destiny helpers. You could push your destiny helpers away through a vendetta.

You're at work and stealing. You may be stealing what would have changed your life forever. You're not faithful to your destiny helper; it may backfire tomorrow. Be careful.

Whoever will move your destiny forward is your destiny helper. God has a way of making divine arrangements for you and your destiny helper. Many life failures occur because destiny helpers do not show up at the right time.

I pray your life will experience the touch of heaven, in

the mighty name of Jesus. Those who will bless you will come into your life, in the mighty name of Jesus.

Your breakthrough may be connected to another person's breakthrough in life. If you do not meet the person you should meet, you cannot do what you're expected to do. Then you cannot fulfill destiny and can't fulfill life. The Almighty has prepared somebody out there to connect you to your destiny. May you find that person, in the name of Jesus.

> *Whoever will move your destiny forward is your destiny helper.*

Any power removing your destiny helpers shall be silenced forever, in the mighty name of Jesus. I pray the enemy will not relocate your destiny helper, in the mighty name of Jesus.

The 38-eight harrowing years of the man by the pool of Bethesda says it all! He is a terrifying picture of a life without destiny helpers. He was in the same condition for a long time. He was probably tired of trying and sat on the same spot, hoping for some luck.

Maybe he had witnessed how other sick, invalid folks left the poolside due to some destiny helpers that hurled them into the yearly troubling of the water. Nothing changed in his life except his increasing age. When nothing changes in your life apart from the calendar year of your birth, it's a clear indication that you lack destiny helpers. God never intends that we should be stagnant in life.

❖ How To Connect With Destiny Helper

- ✓ You must understand your divine assignment; why God brought you here

- ✓ You must repent of every known sin

- ✓ You must pray inquiry prayers

- ✓ You must pray to have your destiny helpers

- ✓ Avoid destiny diluters

Destiny diluters include watching the TV excessively, oversleeping, being an expert at Hollywood and Nollywood series, useless dancing, going to parties, people of destiny don't waste time at parties, and over-relaxation. Others spend long hours on the phone, read useless magazines, and waste time on social media like Facebook and WhatsApp. Facebook has destroyed the spiritual life of many people. That's where they go to church and meet their partners.

There is also the menace of browsing the internet, playing computer games, chatting online (many are now internet addicts), drinking leisurely around, living a life without focus, falling and rising in lust, dating unbelievers, and hiking into relationships.

> *It is a disconnection with a destiny helper when your helper is somewhere, and you're somewhere else.*

Prayers

1) Lord, please, send me destiny helpers, in Jesus' name.

2) Lord, put all my destiny killers like Saul into perpetual sleep, in Jesus' name.

3) Lord, make me an elevator, a destiny helper for somebody else, in Jesus' name.

4) Lord, thank you because you will do more than I ask, think or request, according to Ephesian 3:20, in Jesus' name.

8

Your Destiny Is Your Purpose

Your destiny is your purpose for living. You need to find and fulfill it. Until you start asking yourself critical questions, discovering your purpose for living may be an impossible task. The purpose for living is elusive for those who fail to ask critical questions about their lives. They tend to accept everything as fate; they see everything as a stroke of luck; at best, they see whatever happens as a chance occurrence. Their usual self-defeating conclusion is that people who find their purpose are lucky, whereas others are not so lucky.

Finding the purpose for living has nothing to with luck. God wants everyone to find the purpose He created them. Asking questions has been a proven method of unraveling the mystery of destiny or purpose for living. God always responds to the people who seek the answer to the question of their destiny or purpose for living. Applying James 4: 2 to this context, we can say that we lack revelation of our destiny and get into avoidable struggles because we 'ask not.'

James 4: 2:

Ye lust, and have not: ye kill, and desire to have, and cannot obtain: ye fight and war, yet ye have not, because ye ask not.

God expects us to do more than ask for our daily supplies. He wants us to ask questions about our purpose for living. Getting the answer to the question of our purpose for living is one of the blessings we should enjoy. You need to ask, 'Who am I? Why am I here? Where did I come from? What was I born to do? What can I do? Where do I fit? Why am I different? What is my potential? Where am I going?' These are the critical questions to ask.

> *God has programmed us to find fulfillment in the purpose of our existence.*

There are two persons to ask these questions. First, direct them to yourself as rhetorical questions. You may know some of the answers, and you may have no answer to any. It's not a problem because you have a second person to direct them. The second person to handle the questions is God. He has all the answers to all human questions. It doesn't matter how many questions you have asked to find your purpose for living. If the previous ones haven't led you to its discovery, ask more questions.

A curious observer and experienced counselor tried to help the confused life of a man who lost his business empire and was facing life's puzzles that no professional counselor could solve. The subsequent loss of his family, friends, and heath compounded his problems. He had many questions to ask himself, as his counselors had many more to ask him. To their volume of pertinent questions, they had no answers.

After assessing the situation keenly, the experienced counselor came up with the best approach to handling life's unanswered questions. He suggested an approach everyone seeking to find their purpose for living should emulate. He concludes that all inquiries should be directed to God, either in finding the answer to the purpose for living or in seeking a solution to life's puzzles.

Job 5: 8-9:

8 "But as for me, I would seek God, And to God I would commit my cause-

9 Who does great things, and unsearchable, Marvelous things without number.

The counselor sounded very modest and courteous. He personalized his suggestion by saying, '*But as for me, I would seek God, And to God I would commit my cause.* You have to make finding the answer to your purpose for living a personal responsibility. Others may choose to go through life without thinking twice about why they are here. You can determine to discover your purpose and dare to be different. God has our details as a manufacturer has the details of his product in their manual.

The questions to discover the purpose for living are universal. Every human being should ask them and accept the outcome. Each of us must find answers to the questions of purpose if we will enjoy a meaningful, effective, and fulfilling life. Life makes meaning when it finds and fulfills its purpose.

Living without purpose is frustrating. God has programmed us to find fulfillment in the purpose of our existence. Many negative thoughts like suicide, self-resent, rejection, self-condemnation, alienation, and depression link with the frustration from not finding purpose for living. We can say then that living without purpose puts one's life in danger.

Finding and pursuing the purpose for living can make your life a stereotype.

A man attempted suicide by trying to jump from a ten-story building. Before he did, he was rescued, and he poured out poisonous frustration that pushed his life to the edge. He said: "Let me go. Please let me die," he lamented to his rescuer. With tears flooded eyes, he lamented, 'What was it all for?' Is this all there is? What did I gain? I have everything and yet nothing. Everyone thinks I am a success, but I am a failure.'

He continued: 'I have given everything and received nothing. I made my parents happy/proud; my wife has everything she could desire. My children lack nothing.

My reputation is solid – yet I am empty, depressed, frustrated, and sad. My life has no meaning. I am unfulfilled" Everyone knows what I am, but I still don't know why I am – I'm better dead than alive and not know why.' His lamentation summarizes what purpose means and what it means not to discover it.

❖ Every Day Is an Appointment With Destiny

Purpose finds fulfillment in each day of our lives. Purpose is the answer to the question of our destiny. Once you find your purpose for living, you find the destiny you are created to fulfill.

The myth and misconception that a day will come when purpose will be fulfilled in a dramatic turnaround are misleading. They give us false hope and take our attention away from the daily pursuit of purpose for living. They set our eyes on a day of a big dream or picture looming somewhere ahead. We get set to pursue the day of the manifestation of the picture. We fail to reckon with the significance of each day of our lives.

The truth about the purpose for living is that each day counts. Everyone's purpose for living stretches over the number of days assigned to them. Each day you live without fulfilling or walking in the path of your purpose is a minus to the aggregate days you have. Many people live a whole lifetime in deficit because of the number of wasted days recorded.

The truth about the purpose for living is that each day counts.

Finding and pursuing the purpose for living can make your life a stereotype. Men and women who find their purpose are separated from the crowd. They live each day of their lives in nothing but such as serves their purpose for living.

Every man has been allotted a specific number of days

on earth. You have enough days to find your purpose and fulfill your destiny. In God's wisdom, no one's destiny stretches longer than the number of their days. He has perfectly determined our days and fixed our purpose in each day.

Job 14: 5:

Mortals have a limited life span. You've already decided how long we'll live—
   you set the boundary and no one can cross it. MSG

The above scripture declares that God already knows the number of our days on earth and that none of us will live one minute beyond the time He has already given us. In addition to the fact that God has predetermined the number of our days on earth, He has a purpose and a destiny upon our lives relative to our days.

Technically speaking, our days belong to God! The length of days we are allotted is to fulfill His purpose. Fulfilling His purpose is what our destiny is all about. The only sense we own our days is that we are responsible for ensuring each day serves God's purpose or our destiny fulfillment.

God has pre-determined what He wants us to do each day of our lives.

> **Ephesian 2:10:**
>
> *For we are His workmanship, created in Christ Jesus for good works, which God prepared beforehand that we should walk in them.*

There is a catalog of activities titled '*good works,*' which God had pre-ordained that everyone should live to fulfill. We can't find and fulfill our individual purposes in the catalog of '*good works*' until we embrace Christ. God sent Christ to save us to fulfill the '*good works.*' We can say then that there is nothing like destiny fulfillment outside Christ in the actual sense.

If we can fulfill our destiny without Christ, it is logical to say we don't need Him. But God has planned it so that Christ is the nucleus of anything He wants us to do.

Every day of our lives is a fraction of the total number of days we have to fulfill the '*good works*' God prepared before the world was.

God created us for His purpose; He has a plan and purpose for our lives. He is the Creator, and His creatures are meant to fulfill His purpose. When you know your purpose, it gives meaning to your life every day. John Maxwell, says that 'you find yourself when you discover your purpose.'

> *When you know your purpose, it gives meaning to your life every day.*

Jeremiah 29: 11:

> *For I know the thoughts that I think toward you, says the LORD, thoughts of peace and not of evil, to give you a future and a hope.*

Here are some tips on fulfilling our days and what it is not. It's a checklist to help you assess how you spend your days.

- ✓ **Fulfilling Our Days Is Not Just Exhausting Our Years**

Fulfilling your days does not mean spending between 70 and 80 years or above, according to **Psalm 90:10:** *'The days of our years are threescore years and ten; and if by reason of strength they be fourscore years, yet is their strength labor and sorrow; for it is soon cut off, and we fly away.* It amounts to nothing if all the years don't serve God's purpose.

We care a lot about living up to the number of years God has planned for us. We pray against anything that wants to cut our days short. It is appropriate to care about our days and desire to live through them all. Making each day count by fulfilling our purpose for living is the most important thing God desires in us. In fact, any day lived without fulfilling His purpose is a waste. Wasted days accumulate into wasted weeks, months, and years.

- ✓ **Fulfilling Our Days Is Not Spending Our Years Doing Our Things**

We can spend our days doing our things, pursuing our dreams, and achieving our goals. That's what many motivational speakers teach. They emphasize self-discovery and incite self-energies to pursue self-goals.

The trend and teaching violate God's principle for purpose fulfillment. Anything we do differently from God's purpose for our lives amounts to a failed destiny.

Each day must count toward fulfilling God's purpose. Any day spent without fulfilling God's purpose puts us in danger of answering difficult questions on the Day of Reckoning. Some of us have to work extra hard to redeem some of the wasted days of our lives.

- ✓ **Fulfilling Our Days Means Getting Ready For Good And Bad Times**

Everyone has an appointed time on earth. Job 7: 1 says, Is there not an appointed time to man upon earth? are not his days also like the days of an hireling? (KJV) The word '*time*' in the phrase '…an appointed time…' does not refer to the duration of existence in terms of days, weeks, months, or years. In the original Hebrew text, the word relates to 'host' 'army' or 'war.' So what it means is that for everyone, there is the certainty of troubles, trials, or tribulations like the attack of a host, an army or in an outbreak of war.

The New King James Version (NKJV) renders the phrase '…an appointed time…as 'a time of hard service' or a time of hardship, a tough time, a hard-hitting, life-threatening occurrence. The text reads *"Is there not a time of hard service for man on earth? Are not his days also like the days of a hired man?'* This text means to fulfill our days, we should know that tough times will come, and we rather prepare for them.

Before troubles hit you hard, spend your good days consolidating your stand with God, and develop muscles to withstand the evil days. Living every day like there would never be a challenge makes us unprepared for the unexpected. The outcome can waste the rest days of our lives for lack of preparation.

✓ Fulfilling Our Days Means Being Conscious That Life Is Brief

As a king, an administrator, a ruler, a man of authority over others, a writer, poet, prophet, and warrior, David understood that daily human activities could rob us of many things. Losing the consciousness of the brevity of life is one of the things our daily activities could cost us. David specially prayed that God would help him always to remember that he had a limited lifespan like anyone of us.

His prayer in Psalm 39: 4 says, *"LORD, make me to know my end, And what is the measure of my days, That I may know how frail I am.'* The New Living Translation recast it as

"*Lord, remind me how brief my time on earth will be. Remind me that my days are numbered—how fleeting my life is.*'

We need a reminder that we don't have all the time in the world to do what God has appointed us to do. We must be conscious that fulfilling our purpose or destiny is a time-bound duty and our days are full of fleeting moments. We don't have the luxury of unlimited years on earth. If so much has been left undone despite your daily activities, it's high time you sat down and re-evaluated your schedules as they relate to God's primary assignment for you. Don't be busy doing nothing, and don't do so much fulfilling so little.

✓ Fulfilling Our Days Has Divine Support

God has promised to ensure we fulfill our days. We should seize each day with faith in His promise. We should disengage or bar the devil and his emissaries from each day of our lives. Here is God's promise: '*I will fulfill the number of your days.*' Exodus 23: 26b.

Any day we carelessly yield to human or the devil's control is a loss. God's promise gives us the confidence to face each day and every day of our lives with renewed commitment and excitement. You have God's support to find and fulfill your purpose or destiny each day of your life. Take no chances at all; every day is a brand new opportunity.

✓ Fulfilling Our Days Means Living In Daily Transformation And Achievements

We can spend our days like an evergreen tree. Each day is a step towards the totality of what God wants us to achieve during our lifetime. Isaiah 65: 18-24 captures it all. The text shows that we won't live in vain if we live each day of our lives in God's will and purpose.

"But be ye glad and rejoice for ever in that which I create: for, behold, I create Jerusalem a rejoicing, and her people a joy. **19** And I will rejoice in Jerusalem, and joy in my people: and the voice of weeping shall be no more heard in her, nor the voice of crying. **20** There shall be no more thence an infant of days, nor an old man that hath not filled his days: for the child shall die an hundred years old; but the sinner being an hundred years old shall be accursed. **21** And they shall build houses, and inhabit them; and they shall plant vineyards, and eat the fruit of them. **22** They shall not build, and another inhabit; they shall not plant, and another eat: for as the days of a tree are the days of my people, and mine elect shall long enjoy the work of their hands. **23** They shall not labour in vain, nor bring forth for trouble; for they are the seed of the blessed of the Lord, and their offspring with them. **24** And it shall come to pass, that before they call, I will answer; and while they are yet speaking, I will hear." Isaiah **65:18-24**

❖ **Getting Your Priority Right**

The answer to the demanding and unavoidable daily activities is getting your priority right. God's purpose for your life should top the list of your daily priorities. Every other thing you want to do should answer to fulfilling the purpose.

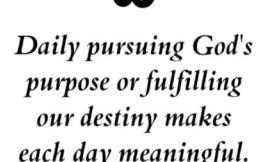

Daily pursuing God's purpose or fulfilling our destiny makes each day meaningful.

Daily pursuing God's purpose or fulfilling our destiny makes each day meaningful. In a general sense, fulfilling our days means realizing or accomplishing something desired, promised, or predicted. Its meaning extends to include success or attainment. But in God's sight, living up to 969 years like Methuselah without accomplishing God's purpose is living in vain.

The renowned German-born physicist, Albert Einstein, said, "A life directed chiefly toward the fulfillment of personal desires will sooner or later always lead to bitter disappointment." Einstein understood that self-pursuit is an obstruction to the ultimate fulfillment of purpose for living.

A popular American motivational speaker, Denis Waitler, says, "It is not in the pursuit of happiness that we find fulfillment, it is in the happiness of pursuit." Waitler's antithesis suggests that we may have to reverse the order of our pursuit to earn true fulfillment.

For most people, a misplaced priority is a reason behind their daily frustrations. God's purpose is at the bottom of their list if it ever makes it to the list. Such a daily to-do list needs a reversal to find fulfillment. God must take the topmost position, and His purpose for us must incontestably stand above all like a pedestal.

A popular American author and coach, Tony Robbins, says, "Success without fulfillment is the ultimate failure." All social instructions like schools, churches, mosques, and other religious houses, families, economic and government systems teach how to succeed. Their flaw is captured in the words of Robbins that one can succeed without being fulfilled. Many successful people are frustrated because their success does not satisfy their inner longing for fulfillment. We find fulfillment in our God-given purpose for living. The fulfillment is our success.

Again, I want to take you back to the importance of asking questions. This time, I have drawn a couple of questions for you to answer. They will help you rearrange your priorities to live a purposeful life.

- ✓ What are your priorities in life?

- ✓ Have you ever spent much time thinking about what you should spend your time on?

- ✓ Do you just go from day to day doing whatever you want and what you feel like doing without asking yourself what you should be doing?

- ✓ What do you do with your time?

The Bible views time as that measurable space where things happen to people. There is, in God's mind, "a time to be born and a time to die, a time to plant and a time to uproot, a time to kill and a time to heal, a time to tear down and a time to build, a time to weep and a time to laugh, a time to mourn and a time to dance, a time to scatter stones and a time to gather them, a time to embrace and a time to refrain, a time to search and a time to give up, a time to keep and a time to throw away, a time to tear and a time to mend, a time to be silent and a time to speak, a time to love and a time to hate, a time for war and a time for peace." (**Ecclesiastes 3:2-8**)

What kind of responsibility do you and I have toward the time we've been given on earth, especially since none of us knows, really, how much time we have on earth? Ecclesiastes 3: 2-8 tells us to be stewards of our time.

- ✓ Are you fulfilling your days or time?

- ✓ Put in another way, does your life count for now and for eternity?

Don't be busy doing nothing, and don't do so much fulfilling so little.

A life of regret is no life at all. Of course, we all have regrets for things we've done, mistakes made, and opportunities lost. But if we make a conscious decision every day to minimize those regrets, we will lead a happier and more fulfilling life. God made us for His purpose, and until you figure that out, life isn't going to make sense. "The purposes of a man's heart are deep waters, but a man of understanding draws them out." (Pro. 20:5)

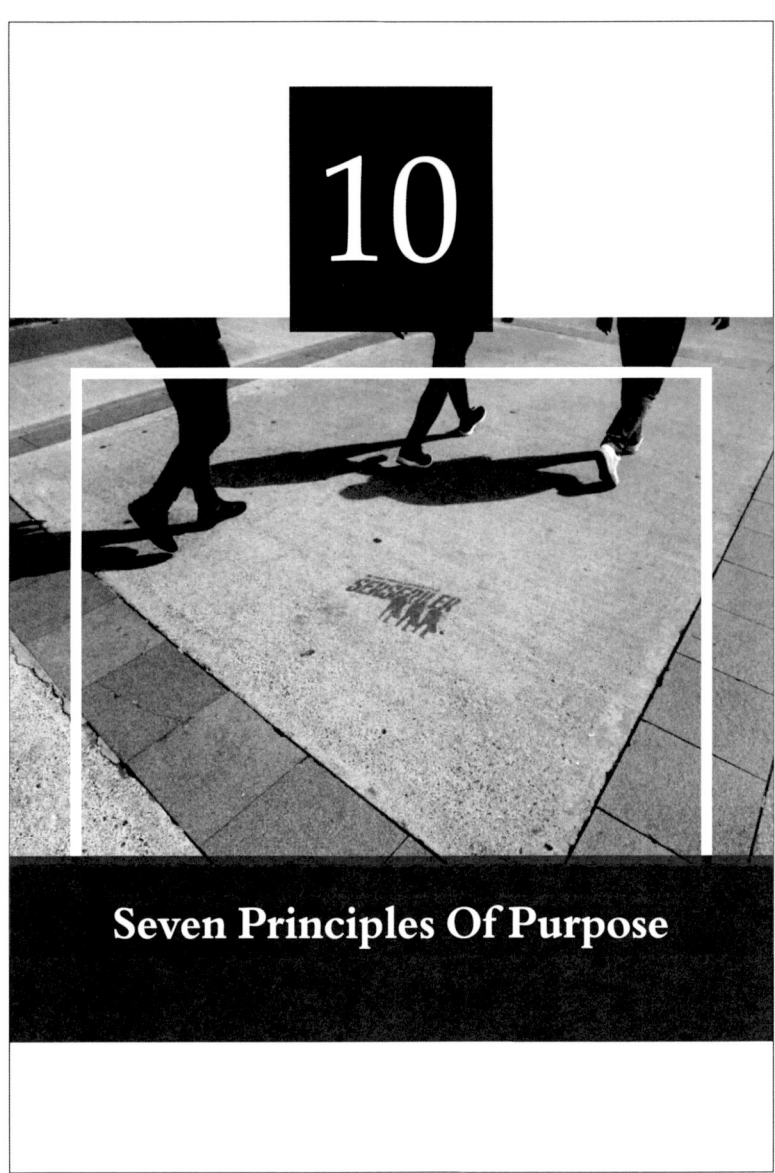

10

Seven Principles Of Purpose

As purpose lives on principles, destiny dies without principles. We can define a principle as many ways as our perceptions can stretch. One of the definitions of 'principle' that has stood the test of time was given by Henri Frédéric Amiel, a Swiss moral philosopher, and poet.

Over a hundred years ago, Henri said, 'He who floats with the current, who does not guide himself according to higher principles, who has no ideal, no convictions- such a man is a mere article of the world's furniture-a thing moved, instead of a living and moving being-an echo, not a voice.'

Henri's submission about a life without principles is very candid and unsparing. Without principles as its guide and anchor, life floats with the currents and is moved instead of moving. Living without principles deprives one of a 'voice,' hence, one becomes a mere echo of those who discover and live by the principles that support their purpose.

I have put together seven principles of purpose to help you live a fulfilled life. They are laws that guide destiny fulfillment because principles are laws. Disobeying the laws for purposeful living guarantees a failed destiny. Ignorantly, people rebel against God and His ways without realizing that their rebellion puts them at variance with the principles for their destiny fulfillment. The seven principles are:

#1. Your Are Designed For A Purpose

> *Our backgrounds could accelerate or retard the process of our destiny fulfillment, but the real raw materials you need are already within you*

This principle implies that you must accept the way you were created with all your peculiarities. When God formed you in your mother's womb, He wired in you everything you need to live and fulfill your destiny. The first attack against this principle is the devil's lie to make you think you lack what it takes to become whom you are destined to become.

You are perfect for your purpose, but the enemy wants you to believe you lack what it takes to function. Naturally, you are a complete package. It doesn't matter the family or religious background into which you were born. What God has put in you to function and fulfill your destiny has nothing to do with your educational, social, or economic background.

Our backgrounds could accelerate or retard the process of our destiny fulfillment, but the real raw materials you need are already within you. Don't let your background put your back on the ground. At birth, God has put in you certain qualities and characteristics to enable you to perform His intended purpose. You are a complete and perfect original product. Don't let anything or anyone cause you to malfunction.

Psychologists recognize the problem of self-hatred in people. They perceive it as a feeling of inadequacy. That is exactly what the problem is. When you don't embrace and appreciate who you are as you are, there is a tendency for you to wish you were somebody else. With that negative thought, negative energies are released within you that inhibit your ability to function as you should.

Comparison is one of the commonest reasons people have self-hate and cannot function in their natural abilities. The Bible says such a comparison that deprives us of becoming the best we are designed to be is unwise. 'But they, measuring themselves by themselves, and comparing themselves among themselves, are not wise.' 2 Corinthians 10: 12.

Everything you are, everything you naturally have, and everything you inherently are - everything is necessary for you to fulfill your purpose. It includes your height, race, skin color, language, physical features, and intellectual capacity. Never try to become like someone else – what you are is important and essential to why you are here in the world.

In the new birth experience of everyone who accepts Jesus as Lord and Savior, God reclaims what is rightfully His. The Christian's salvation or new birth experience does not throw away their natural endowments. God didn't throw away Moses' skills and talents at the burning bush encounter.

Before then, Moses demonstrated skills, talents, and enthusiasms in ministering deliverance to his oppressed people. He displayed a fight against injustice in defense of his people, and he introduced an alternative dispute resolution process between two Hebrews in a conflict with each other.

Never try to become like someone else

When we become born again, God renews, redirects, and redeploys our natural endowments. He did the same thing for Moses.

Exodus 2: 11-13 & 3: 10:

11 Now it came to pass in those days, when Moses was grown, that he went out to his brethren and looked at their burdens. And he saw an Egyptian beating a Hebrew, one of his brethren.

12 So he looked this way and that way, and when he saw no one, he killed the Egyptian and hid him in the sand.

13 And when he went out the second day, behold, two Hebrew men were fighting, and he said to the one who did the wrong, "Why are you striking your companion?"

10. "Come now, therefore, and I will send you to Pharaoh that you may bring My people, the children of Israel, out of Egypt."

As Moses was equipped for his purpose, so are you.

Prayer:

1. Confess your acceptance and confidence in whom God created you to be by repeating the words of the Psalmist: 'I will praise You, for I am

fearfully and wonderfully made; …Psalm 139:14a

2. Father, all that I have lost (opportunities, unction, promotion, favor, etc.), let me recover them again, in the name of Jesus.

3. According to **Joel 2:25-26**, Oh God, please begin to restore to me the lost years of my life, in the name of Jesus.

#2. Purpose Is Individual

You are the way you are because of why you are here in the world. Moses viewed his speech impediment as a hindrance until he saw the bigger picture of God's purpose for his life. In the bigger picture, God made him a 'god' to Pharaoh and appointed Aaron, his brother, as 'his prophet.'

In God's ultimate purpose for Moses, He was created to walk in the majesty of a deity who would need the service of a mouthpiece as a prophet. He sure didn't have to be an orator after all; the glory and majesty God conferred on him required the service of a prophet as a Personal Assistant (PA).

Exodus 7: 1-2:

1 So the LORD said to Moses: "See, I have made you as God to Pharaoh, and Aaron your brother shall be your prophet.

2 "You shall speak all that I command you. And Aaron your brother shall speak to Pharaoh to send the children of Israel out of his land.

Purpose is an individual affair. What makes you the individual you are is what you need to fulfill your purpose. A stereo system includes a turntable, a cassette player, and a CD player to fulfill different purposes that are not interchangeable. The CD players cannot play a cassette tape – their purposes are individual and separate, though they are similar. Their uniqueness doesn't make the various parts unequal' they are just different because of the functions they perform.

God needs you because your purpose is unique. No one has your fingerprint, personality, and the particular combination of natural skills and talents.

In essence, there is something you came to this planet to do that the world needs in this generation.

Peter and Paul were two great leaders in church history. They were called into a large loop of God's Kingdom service, but they both understood their individual purposes to fulfill. Peter was an apostle to the Jews, while Paul was an apostle to the Gentiles. No one can take your place or purpose, and there is no substitute for you.

Galatians 2:7-8:

7 But on the contrary, when they saw that the gospel for the uncircumcised had been committed to me, as the gospel for the circumcised was to Peter

8 (for He who worked effectively in Peter for the apostleship to the circumcised also worked effectively in me toward the Gentiles),

Moses' rod would not work for Joshua. As a different individual with a different purpose to fulfill, God's dealing with him was different from Moses' experience. While God gave Moses a shepherd's rod, He gave Joshua the book of the Law for his meditation, confession, and application.

Joshua 1:3, 8:

3 "Every place that the sole of your foot will tread upon I have given you, as I said to Moses.

8 "This Book of the Law shall not depart from your mouth, but you shall meditate in it day and night, that you may observe to do according to all that is written in it. For then you will make your way prosperous, and then you will have good success.

Everyone's difference finds an appropriate connection with their destiny fulfillment. Proverbs 18:16 says, "A man's gift maketh room for him and bringeth him before great men."

Pray this prayer with faith: Father, let my gift start manifesting to make room for me, in the name of Jesus.

#3. Purpose Is Often Multi-dimensional

Just as purpose is specific to a particular individual or product, it may be varied and numerous. For example, the sun serves the following purposes: (i) To separate the day from the night, (ii) To mark the seasons, days, and years, (iii) To govern the day (iv) To separate light from darkness and (v) To give light to the earth.

Genesis 1:14-18:

14 Then God said, "Let there be lights in the firmament of the heavens to divide the day from the night; and let them be for signs and seasons, and for days and years;

15 "and let them be for lights in the firmament of the heavens to give light on the earth"; and it was so.

16 Then God made two great lights: the greater light to rule the day, and the lesser light to rule the night. He made the stars also.

17 God set them in the firmament of the heavens to give light on the earth,

18 and to rule over the day and over the night, and to divide the light from the darkness. And God saw that it was good.

Trees give oxygen, shade, and fruit. Animals provide food and clothing. Men and Women assume the varied roles of spouses, parents, workers, church members, and friends.

Moses had a variety of purposes to fulfill:

(i) He was a spokesman for God to the Pharaoh of Egypt (Exodus 3-13).

(ii) He was a warrior of God whose uplifted hands brought victory over the Amalekites (Exodus 17:8-13)

(iii) He was a priest of God who mediated between God and His People (Exodus 19-31)

(iv) He was a lawgiver of God, who authored the first five books of the Bible.

His ability to perform the demanding multiplicity of purpose was made possible by the interdependent nature of assignments.

He needed Joshua, Jethro, and others to help him carry out his God-given purpose.

God's gifting of articulation in T.D. Jakes' life as a preacher, author, TV host, movie producer, and speaker has afforded him multiple income streams. You may be equipped with multiple gifts for a multi-dimensional purpose. Recognize and release them in the direction of your purpose for living.

Pray like this:

- ✓ Father, make me a river, not a reservoir, in the name of Jesus.

- ✓ Father, help me discover other areas where I can be used or useful, in the name of Jesus.

- ✓ Father, bless me so I can be a blessing to others, in the name of Jesus.

God wants to deliver His services to humanity and draw His blessings to you through your gifts.

#4. Purpose Cannot Be Fulfilled In Isolation

Nothing exists for itself; everything is related to something else. Purpose is interdependent. God made the sun the greater light and the moon the lesser light. The sun rules the day, while the moon governs the night. To fulfill its purpose, the moon must always remain in a position to catch the sun's light and reflect it to the earth.

Take a car battery. The purpose of a battery is to store energy until it is needed. If the battery is never placed in a position that requires its stored energy, it cannot fulfill its purpose. But without the ignition key, the battery cannot send the stored power. Without the battery, the engine, the wheels, or the car cannot fulfill their purposes. Everything needs something, just as everyone needs someone.

Romans 12:4-5:

4 For as we have many members in one body, but all the members do not have the same function,

5 so we, being many, are one body in Christ, and individually members of one another.

1 Cor. 12: 24-27:

24 but our presentable parts have no need. But God composed the body, having given greater honor to that part which lacks it,

25 that there should be no schism in the body, but that the members should have the same care for one another.

26 And if one member suffers, all the members suffer with it; or if one member is honored, all the members rejoice with it.

27 Now you are the body of Christ, and members individually.

The interrelatedness of the Church is part of God's purpose. He gives to each member a task that contributes to the Church's overall purpose, thereby allowing the Church to grow in love and build "itself up in love, as each part does its work."

> *Purpose is an individual affair. What makes you the individual you are is what you need to fulfill your purpose.*

Ephesians 4: 15-16:

15 but, speaking the truth in love, may grow up in all things into Him who is the head--Christ—

16. from whom the whole body, joined and knit together by what every joint supplies, according to the effective working by which every part does its share, causes growth of the body for the edifying of itself in love.

For God to fulfill His purpose, He needs your cooperation. Just suppose the tree on which Jesus was crucified refused to become a tree, or Joseph of Arimathea did not purchase the tomb in which Jesus was destined to lay. Imagine how the gospel narrative would have changed. Your purpose is designed to affect history within and beyond your generation.

Prayers:

1. Father, help me to make impact; and connect me to my destiny helpers, in the mighty name of Jesus. Psalm 46:1," God is our refuge, and strength, the very present help in trouble."

2. Pray that all our entangled soldiers, our derailed and distracted 'Moses' and 'Demas,' would hear the alarm and the battle cry, and they will return to base, not fearing the wrath of their Pharaohs, in the mighty name of Jesus.

3. If you're not yet a victim of this temptation, you need to pray for the grace never to take the adversary for granted. Paul said, 'we should not be ignorant of his (Satan's) devises. The antidote to distraction is Discipline!

#5. Purpose Is Permanent

Proverbs 19: 21 tells us that 'Many are the plans in a man's heart, but it is the Lord's purpose that prevails.'

Plans may change, but purpose is constant.

Once a manufacturer designs, produces, and markets a product that fulfills a certain purpose, he does not change that purpose because a consumer doesn't like the way it works.

God promised Abraham and Sarah a son. Sarah tried to help God achieve that purpose by giving Hagar to Abraham. Hagar conceived and bore a son, Ishmael. Abraham tried to make Ishmael the promised son. But God did not accede to his wishes.

As revealed in His covenant with Abraham and Sarah, His purpose was the birth of the promised son.

Genesis 17:17-22:

17 Then Abraham fell on his face and laughed, and said in his heart, "Shall a child be born to a man who is one hundred years old? And shall Sarah, who is ninety years old, bear a child?"

18 And Abraham said to God, "Oh, that Ishmael might live before You!"

19 Then God said: "No, Sarah your wife shall bear

you a son, and you shall call his name Isaac; I will establish My covenant with him for an everlasting covenant, and with his descendants after him.

20 "And as for Ishmael, I have heard you. Behold, I have blessed him, and will make him fruitful, and will multiply him exceedingly. He shall beget twelve princes, and I will make him a great nation.

21 "But My covenant I will establish with Isaac, whom Sarah shall bear to you at this set time next year."

22 Then He finished talking with him, and God went up from Abraham.

Prayer: Father, help me to not give birth to Ismael out of impatience, in Jesus' name.

If you try to do what someone else is gifted at, you will only be frustrated and stressed, and it will seriously limit your abilities to do your best for God. *You must run your own race!* Romans 12:5 "Since we find ourselves fashioned into all these excellently formed and marvelously functioning parts in Christ Body, let's just go ahead and be what we were made to be."

#6. Purpose Is Resilient

Once a purpose for a product is established and developed, No amount of problems with the manufacturing process will change the product's purpose. Each difficulty that seeks to hinder progress toward completing a product is used to learn more about the product. The journey may include bumps and detours, but eventually, it will come to the desired end.

Habakkuk 2: 3:

For the vision is yet for an appointed time; But at the end it will speak, and it will not lie. Though it tarries, wait for it; Because it will surely come, It will not tarry.

Purpose transforms mistakes into miracles and disappointments into testimonies. Before he met Christ on the road to Damascus, Saul or Paul was a very talented person.

(i) As an organizer, he systematically organized persecution against the Church in Jerusalem.

(ii) He received letters from appropriate authorities – Acts 8:3, 9:1

(iii) He was a leader, as evident in his role in the stoning of Stephen (Acts 22:20 Acts 7:58; 8:1)

(iv) He was a skilled tentmaker who liked to work with his hands (Acts 18:3)

(v) He was a communicator - by speaking and writing, Paul declared what he believed. He wrote over 60% of the New Testament.

Yes, God changed his name but not his purpose. Your past does not hinder God's purpose. Nothing you have done can cancel your purpose. He turned a coward (Gideon) into a mighty leader (Judges 6-8); a murderer (Moses) into a mighty deliverer (Ex. 3). He also turned a prostitute (the Samaritan woman) into a preacher (John 4:1-42). Imagine what he can make of you. You are not too old to resume your purpose. The world is waiting for you to produce your purpose.

#7. Purpose Is Universal

Nothing is created without a purpose behind it. God also chose the mosquito and designed everything it needs to fulfill its reason for being. We fail to appreciate its purpose because of our narrow view of it as a malaria vector. Nothing is outside God's universal purpose.

Whenever this commonness of purpose is not recognized, death occurs.

The Dead Sea is a good example of the inevitable death that occurs when purpose is not fulfilled. The Dead Sea collects water from the Sea of Galilee and the Jordan River, but it doesn't let it out. It contains no plant or marine life – no fish there. – It's too salty to sustain life.

The Sea is dead because it shares in the universality of purpose but fails to live up to that purpose.

God needs you because your purpose is unique.

The tragedy of the Dead Sea is illustrative of our lives – He already predestinated us and chose us to be conformed to the image of His Son. He set Christ as our destination and then backed us up and started us on the journey toward that desired end

No matter how your life started or how bad it has been, you are not a mistake. God intended for you to live, both physically and spiritually. He would not have allowed you to be born if you had not been included in His universal purpose. You are necessary; you are essential.

Prayers:

1. Wisdom to understand God's times, seasons, and purposes for my life, come upon me from today, in Jesus' name.

2. The grace to start well and finish strong in life, fall upon me from today, in Jesus' name.

3. The grace to be a voice, not a noise, an asset and relevant to my generation, come upon me, in Jesus' name.

The message is for us to understand the basic principles of purpose and how they help in destiny fulfillment. We need to recognize and apply them to guide and direct our paths. "Before formed you in the womb I knew you, before you were born I set you apart (Jeremiah 1:5).

The man or woman who wants to fulfill his or her days will journey through life in partnership with God through the Holy Spirit. God is faithful, and He will always do His part as He said in Exodus 23:26: "There shall nothing cast their young, nor be barren, in thy land: the number of thy days I will fulfill;"

I decree upon your life that you will not die young; none will die before their time in your household; and you will fulfill your days, in Jesus' name.

However, you must live carefully in these evil times. Live as wise, not as unwise. Make the most of every opportunity. Understand the Lord's will in everything you do. **Ephesians 5:17** says: "Therefore do not be foolish but understand what the Lord's will is." Most of God's will is written in the Scriptures. God will never lead you to do anything contrary to His revealed will in the Word.

Allow God to have His way. Let Him change your plans where He wishes. **Proverbs 16: 9** says, "A man's heart deviseth his way: but the Lord directeth his steps." God can overrule your plans at any time, so allow Him. He knows better than you about how best to allocate your time.

Prayers:

1. declare that my dream will not die, in the mighty name of Jesus.

2. Every evil agenda or covenant working against my life and my good dreams is cancelled by the Blood of

Jesus.

3. Every dream killer in my life, I arrest you, in the mighty name of Jesus.

4. Fire of jealousy raging in my life and dreams, be quenched, in the mighty name of Jesus.

5. Every conspiracy against my life is scattered, in Jesus' name.

6. Father let your Word prosper and find fulfillment in my life, cancel every evil verdict against my life, in the mighty name of Jesus.

7. Father, remove every old thing blocking the manifestation of new things in my life, in the mighty name of Jesus.

8. Lord, order my steps this year, in Jesus' name.

9. Father, let me be at the right place at the right time doing the right thing throughout this year, in Jesus' name.

10. My legs, hear the Word of God: 'from January to December, you shall carry me into my breakthroughs,' in Jesus' name.

11. I decree that the ground where I stand, where I live, walk, work, worship is consecrated unto the Lord, in Jesus' name.

12. This year, I shall tread upon serpents and scorpions and nothing shall by any means hurt me, in Jesus' name.

13. Father, make my feet like that of a deer and set me high upon the Rock, in Jesus' name.

14. My feet shall carry me to high and far places to possess this year, in Jesus' name.

15. Father, help me to walk worthy of you and be fruitful in every good work, in Jesus' name.

16. I reject and renounce the spirit of wrong location and wrong vocation, in Jesus name.

17. Iron gate leading to the city of my breakthroughs, I am coming, open of your own accord, in Jesus' name.

18. God of time and chance, carry my feet into divine opportunities this year, in Jesus' name.

19. Father, have mercy and make it impossible for anyone in my family including me to walk into hell fire, in

Jesus' name.

20. Thank you, Father, for leading me in the right way that I should go this year, in Jesus' name.